THE STORY OF THE WHITE EAGLE LODGE

The Story of
the White Eagle Lodge

THE WHITE EAGLE PUBLISHING TRUST
NEW LANDS : LISS : HAMPSHIRE : ENGLAND

First published October 1986

Text matter by Ylana Hayward, Joan Hodgson, Colum Hayward
(editor) and other members of White Eagle's family. The whole
based on research by Alison Innes.

The extract from Ursula Roberts' autobiography, LIVING IN TWO
WORLDS (1984), is reproduced by kind permission of the author
and her publishers, Regency Press. The photograph on p. 17 is
copyright BBC Hulton Picture Library, and those on pp. 40 & 41
copyright *Psychic News* as well as that of the Celtic cross (carved by
Ivan Cooke) on the front cover. The picture on p. 52 is by Donald
Eades.

British Library Cataloguing in Publication Data
The Story of the White Eagle Lodge.
1. White Eagle Lodge
133.9   BF1283.W54/

ISBN 0-85487-071-7

Set in 10 on 12pt Baskerville by
Goodfellow and Egan Phototypesetting Ltd., Cambridge
and printed in Great Britain by Oxford University Press

Contents

Dedication

LOOKING back over the fifty years of the Lodge work to produce this brief history, we find many memories come to us, tumbling over each other in their efforts to establish their own place in the long story. Most of all, our memories of friends who, over the years and in many different ways, have made their own special contribution to the building of the White Eagle Lodge – sometimes perhaps without even realising how their loving action would materially affect the whole course of the work. So many memories of kind deeds and faithful service; such an array of kind faces come to mind, very particularly those who just 'kept on keeping on', bringing their own special qualities of spirit to White Eagle, and without whom there would be no White Eagle Lodge. Many are now in the world of spirit, but they are still part of the big White Eagle family: still working with us, ever more closely, as the bridge of light between the two worlds becomes stronger through our aspiration and meditation.

We remember you all with great affection and we dedicate this book to you in love and thankfulness.

Woodcut by 'Swoz' (F. E. Swarsbrick) from an edition of ANGELUS. *The initial on page 1, by the same artist, is from the book* THE WHITE BROTHERHOOD

Introduction

This is the Golden Jubilee story of an organisation founded at the instigation of a group of brothers – we shall call them the brothers of the Great White Light – in the world of spirit. If it had a subtitle, it would probably be 'guidance, vision, brotherhood', for that defines the relationship between those who do the work on earth and those who direct it in the higher world. The guidance should be evident throughout the book, and also the vision which, given to them by the brothers above, the work's earthly leaders have demonstrated. The brotherhood is the ideal which, set before them by the brothers of the Light, the followers of the teaching seek to put into practice, for it is only by the practice of brotherhood that anything at all is created, as far as this work is concerned.

White Eagle is the spokesman for this group of brothers in the world of spirit. He is our teacher, but though he brings with him the gentle personality of an Indian chief, his name simply means a wise teacher, and there are times when it is better not to think of the individual, but of the group above who guide and watch over us.

White Eagle's medium, for all of her earthly life, was our founder Minesta, Mrs Grace Cooke, now herself in the world of spirit with Brother Faithful her husband, and like White Eagle very, very active in the guidance of the work at the intuitive level. We call her Minesta in this book, which was the name she had when in an incarnation in the Mayan civilization. That story is told in her book, THE ILLUMINED ONES. Brother Faithful is the name White Eagle gave to Ivan Cooke in this life, and it so suits him that we use it here, and ask for the patience and the understanding of those who would have preferred earthly names to be used, as they read this book.

Minesta's qualities as a leader, her courage and her fidelity to the work she was given to do, will we hope be evident to all who read this book. We of her family, who have compiled it, remember her above all as a mother, and know that the love she showed to each of us was the same as she showed to each of the members of her wider 'family' in the Lodge. 'Above all', we once wrote,

> White Eagle and the Brotherhood wanted the teaching to remain always simple and pure. He wanted the work to be built on a loving family spirit of helpfulness, kindness and sympathetic understanding of each other's difficulties, not only practical difficulties, but the soul struggles which beset each one of us according to our karma. Often even her closest family

could not understand at the time why Minesta acted in a certain way, or made certain decisions, but we soon learnt to respect these decisions and follow her guidance . . . Minesta's 'bright eyes' looking into the future enabled her to foresee the pitfalls likely to arise through the weaknesses in human nature, and guard against them.

Joan Hodgson, 'Personal Recollections of Minesta and White Eagle',
STELLA POLARIS, *October–November 1980*

Brother Faithful spent all his life, from the time he met her, by Minesta's side, protecting her and enabling her always to give of her best. His untiring work, and the strength of his personality, was as important as hers in the building of the Lodge as a group of servers, students of the Light, and his wisdom and humour gave it a character all will remember with very great affection. His special contribution (besides being a wonderful healer and sensitive himself) was in getting White Eagle's teaching into print: he was the editor of all the early books and also of ANGELUS, the Lodge magazine, and its successor STELLA POLARIS.

This book is a rather personal story of the Lodge. Though we hope that friends who have newly been introduced to the teaching will enjoy it, some will take a little time to adjust to the way of looking at life that the book demonstrates. A Lodge is a gatehouse to the mansion which lies beyond, but it is also a place where those on their journey through life may come for refreshment and, in resting, find greater insight. We welcome all who read this book into our Lodge and pray that they may realise the loving acceptance of our teacher.

1

Burstow and Pembroke Hall

THIS WORK was planned a long time ago. You yourselves have been drawn to it by links of karma. Although everyone likes to feel that he is wholly independent, actually no soul is wholly free. For it is tied by fine links to its own past, and also to its future. This is how you have all been drawn to this work.

Whenever a small group commences this kind of work the White Brotherhood above watch over it. This happened with the Christian brotherhoods of long ago who also worked unknown and unseen. They persisted bravely and faithfully over the years so that all mankind today has much for which to thank these Christian brothers. They gave their life, their service to humanity. So may it be with you.

White Eagle's address at the Silver Jubilee Service,
London Lodge, 22 February 1961

 HERE is really no beginning, and no end. But we have chosen to tell a chapter, for it is the Golden Jubilee of the earthly commencement of our work, and so we look back fifty years, to 1936. Or rather, we look a few years earlier, for the Lodge was conceived not in Kensington that year, but at Burstow Manor in Surrey, a little previously.

Grace Cooke (White Eagle used to call her 'Brighteyes' and later 'Minesta', the name we shall use in this book) was first introduced to Burstow in 1929, when her help and that of Brother Faithful (Ivan Cooke) was sought by its owner to help in the release of an earthbound soul: 'as sorrowful an earthbound soul as ever I met' – so Brother Faithful later described her. Happiness came out of sorrow: the story of the release of Mary is movingly told by Brother Faithful in THE HEAVENS ARE RINGING (1930). Subsequently Minesta was called there again – this time to help, through her psychic gift, in the search for a 'buried treasure' which Burstow's owner, a Mrs Trotter, had been assured was buried there. Time has revealed that treasure to be of a spiritual rather than an earthly nature; for out of the spiritual contact which was made through that work, and the work with Mary, grew the vision of Burstow as a healing and retreat centre. As far back as 1924 Mrs Trotter had been told from spirit that 'this old house, built in a place of prayer and sanctity, had been chosen as the centre for a brotherhood yet to be formed, from which would emanate influence and teaching which would eventually become worldwide'. And in 1929 White Eagle himself had told her that it was a place of spiritual peace, one of the special centres of Britain: 'one for them [the spirit world] to use for the purpose they know of. It is only in this place that the seed can be sown'.

And so it came about that in 1932 Burstow was leased for an initial three years, to be used as a centre for healing and retreat. Just about this time a man and his wife had come to White Eagle in dire need – he was unemployed, with a little family to support – and it was partly to help them that the venture was embarked upon, for they were installed to manage the home, leaving White Eagle's medium free (or so she hoped) to do the spiritual work.

Burstow was a little hamlet, lying just off the Brighton road, about thirty miles from London. Rather as with New Lands today, as soon as one turned off the busy main road into the little lane leading to the old house, with the church by its side, the old rectory, and a few cottages which comprised the hamlet, there was a feeling of remoteness from the world, and a peace. It was almost like going into another age. Part of the house was really old, with massive oak beams and a great fireplace which took enormous logs. You could sit right inside this next to the fire and roast comfortably; or, if you chose, come out from this inglenook and freeze. The rest was of more recent date with less atmosphere, though more convenient. We remember a vast kitchen range which consumed coal at a great rate – but coal was only 30s 0d a ton then. A path ran round the boundary of the lawn and flowerbeds, where monks in brown habit from another age could be seen with inner vision, walking as if in prayer. We came to know the gentle presences of Amyas, Clement and Joseph quite well, and called the path 'The Monks' Walk'. Many years later, when our first sight of New Lands was of green lawns bordered by a sheltered walk, we felt at once we had come home to Burstow. It was 'The Monks' Walk' all over again.

From 1929 or before, White Eagle had been speaking about the White Brotherhood (as he then called it) in the world of light, and of how earthly centres of the Brotherhood would be established in various parts of the world. He said that certain men and women, linked consciously or unconsciously with the Lodge of the Brotherhood in the world above, would in due course be drawn together to form the nuclei of groups, drawn together for the purpose of working with the power of good- or God-thought – the power of the Light – for the welfare of mankind, and to bring about the unfoldment of man's consciousness.

If there could come a unification of these men of goodwill, their formation into Groups or Lodges [White Eagle indicated,] then,

The opening of Burstow Manor, 25 March 1933. On Minesta's right is Estelle Stead; flanking the group are Joan and Ylana. Behind, in the doorway, centre, is W.R. Bradbrook, who took down all the Conan Doyle messages and behind and between Minesta and Miss Stead is 'Uncle Frank' Wharhirst, Minesta's brother-in-law.

MAN
MADE PERFECT

The Science of Spiritual Evolution

BEING A SERIES OF TEACHINGS SENT BY
THE WHITE BROTHERHOOD

THROUGH THE HAND OF
MABEL BEATTY

LONDON: RIDER & CO.
PATERNOSTER HOUSE, E.C.

Title page of Mrs Beatty's book

The Bulletin des Polaires, *October 1931, featuring the work with Conan Doyle*

instead of individual contact with the light, would be that more powerful thing, a collective reception. Such groups in turn would then serve as distributors for the Light – that great White Light which at the Source is the very breath and being of Christ . . . and to such service his medium and others might find themselves called, albeit in humble capacity.

Ivan Cooke, THE WHITE BROTHERHOOD

In these early years confirmation of the existence of the Brotherhood in the world of spirit came from a completely separate source. There was published at the end of 1929 a book entitled MAN MADE PERFECT, which (as many readers will know) consisted of teachings received from the White Brotherhood through the hand of Mabel Beatty. The teachings contained in the book and those given by White Eagle were so similar that Minesta was invited to join Mrs Beatty's group, and she attended regularly in 1930–31. On 27 January 1931 Sir Arthur Conan Doyle spoke through Minesta for the first time, at a small gathering arranged by the Polaire Brotherhood of Paris and the Conan Doyle family. The Polaires' instructions, received through a mathematical means of divination, were remarkable in their correspondences with what was being received mediumistically in England regarding the work of the White Brotherhood (the Polaires had formed in 1929 and their teaching was that of true brotherhood through the realisation of the spirit within). Following White Eagle's guidance, Minesta and Brother Faithful were initiated into the Brotherhood in Paris later, in 1931, though it was not until February 1934 (after much testing in the area of human relationships, and what Minesta was later to describe as 'the deepest spiritual suffering' (STELLA POLARIS, 1963), which caused the temporary closure of the home) that definite instructions were received from the Brotherhood above that a Lodge of the Polaires was to be formed at Burstow. An emissary came from Paris to assist in the formation of this group, which met regularly from the summer of that year onwards.

A word now about those who gathered about White Eagle at Burstow in those days. In the early 1930s, White Eagle was becoming known and loved by an increasing number of people through his talks to audiences at the Marylebone Spiritualist Association (now the S.A.G.B.); at the London Spiritual Mission in Pembridge Place (founded by Ernest and Percy Beard, to whose son, Paul, we shall refer later); and at the W.T. Stead Library and Bureau in Westminster. Here his medium worked with and for W. T. Stead's daughter, Estelle, and gave much remarkable evidence and comfort and guidance to those who came privately for help. It was at the Stead Library that the original group met who had sought Minesta's help in contacting Sir Arthur Conan Doyle after his passing. The publication of the messages from Sir Arthur in the book THY

KINGDOM COME also served to focus attention on the work at Burstow. Subsequently Estelle Stead became one of the Burstow brothers, and was on the platform at the opening of the Lodge in 1936. It was from these contacts that the little group gathered round the family were drawn – in addition, of course, to those living locally who attended the Sunday services at the Manor.

The original core of brothers numbered just twelve. They met every week at Burstow and sometimes at the Stead Library as well. But the group grew fast: by the end of the first year, 1934, there were nearly thirty of them; and by the end of 1935, over fifty (including a group who met in Edinburgh, as we shall see). We remember many of these early brothers with special affection: their service was not necessarily greater than those who have come after, but their significance is great, and a few of them are alive – and serving – today, while others surely work with us from the other side of life, giving their support still to the work of the Brotherhood.

One of the early brothers: Constance Malcolm, 'Blue Star'

Brother Faithful describes Burstow in THE HEAVENS ARE RINGING as 'a wonderful old place of great oaken beams, of quaint passages and flights of unexpected stairs, and windows opening to views of lawns and lake or green-clad trees'. We remember vividly the chorus of nightingales through warm May nights, and the glow-worms which picked out the path for us with their bright gleam. The chief 'view of lawns and lake' was from an upper room which had been a billiard and play room but was now transformed into a chapel, that chapel which will always be remembered because it was there that the first seeds of the Brotherhood work were sown.

> The Brethren will not forget the little chapel. Chilly or overheated, exuberantly draughty or sweltering under the sun, in memory it stands out as wholly beautiful, gracious, wholly peaceful. We remember the lilies upon the altar, the soft lights above, the seated circle of the Brethren. Outside perhaps it was a summer's night, and dusk was gathering; there would come the scent of trodden grass, of flowers, the hush of nature wherein are interwoven multitudinous sounds of breathings, yet which holds in itself a silence profound. It was then as if the Brethren were joined in an at-one-ment with all creation – with grass and flower, bush and tree, bird and beast, with the soft night winds and starlight. Then, indeed, the Brotherhood embraced all living things – and reached out and found very close and real those mystical and magical powers which encompassed us.
>
> *Ivan Cooke, in* THE WHITE BROTHERHOOD

Burstow Manor. The projecting window at the right hand end of the building is that of the chapel

Early in 1935 came another period of spiritual trials and human difficulties, as a result of which the English Brotherhood became completely independent of the French group. The significance of this is considerable, for with the coming of the Second World War and the 'years of fire' so long predicted by the Wise Ones, and in

Minesta in the garden at Burstow, with one of our earliest brothers, Anne Bowen, 'Mauris'

The Brotherhood altar at Burstow

particular the occupation of Paris by the German army, the group in Paris was no longer able to operate. It seems to us, looking back, that there was a gradual transference of power from the original Polaire group to the Brotherhood in England. The latter was able to work ceaselessly through the war years, unlike its parent.

After the break with the French group the name of the English one was changed, under White Eagle's guidance, to the White Brotherhood or the Star Brotherhood.

The time at Burstow was a deeply testing one for everyone – there were manifold difficulties, much pain, as well as great happiness and remarkable spiritual illumination. It turned out to be a training ground where much was learnt and much experience gained. Looking back on the problems, one gets the overall impression that they all had a very definite purpose. The association with the Polaire Brotherhood was apparently not meant to last, but it brought the little English Brotherhood under the strong Polaire Star. The vicissitudes in the administration of Burstow caused the running of the Brotherhood (and later the Lodge) to be brought entirely under spiritual guidance, not the guidance of any earthly committee or council. Further, the tests and trials rallied the faithful to the centre of the work. And at the earthly level much was learnt about the practical running of a spiritual centre.

When the lease expired in the autumn of 1935 it was believed that the Brotherhood would be able to buy Burstow. At least, such were the earthly hopes, but they were soon to be dashed. Painful it was, once more, and yet White Eagle was already guiding our thoughts towards the London centre. 'First the London centre, then the country home . . .' he said prophetically (although Burstow was of course the birthplace). It was a surprising direction, yet intrinsic to the Lodge's growth. As to Burstow: it is now a mile from Gatwick Airport, and right under the take-off path.

> When the time came to leave the Manor House – rather a saddening task – the chapel was dismantled; and strange it was to note how even prior to that dismantling the power and sanctity seemed to fade away. At the last meeting of the Brotherhood it was, as ever, its sanctuary and shrine; it became no more than any other room when stripped, and that which had sanctified it was withdrawn into the invisible.
>
> Then followed a difficult time. We had been instructed to seek premises in town, and what was needed seemed almost unattainable. Many months expired, during which some few of the Brethren held their Lodge in the home of two of the Brethren, which meetings served to keep the flame alight.
>
> *Ivan Cooke, in* THE WHITE BROTHERHOOD

The two were Hilda and James Pritchard, known in the Brotherhood as 'Ruth' and 'James'. We name them, and with great love, because they were later to become truly pillars of the Lodge, and their contribution to White Eagle's work in service at all levels is incalculable. Happily their daughter is still with us, though one of our earliest members.

Then at last we heard of premises in Kensington.

That White Eagle guided us to the premises is literally true; because after we had spent some months looking for the desired accommodation he quietly sent a message advising us to go without delay to the house agent (the agent was specified) to enquire for vacant premises.

Having learnt by this time to act on this inner voice, we lost no time. Sure enough, the house agent had, only an hour before we arrived, received notification that Pembroke Hall, Kensington, had become vacant and could be leased at a suitable rental. On inspecting the premises we found ourselves somewhat dismayed. The property was in a bad condition, requiring rather extensive repairs and redecoration throughout. However, as these were the premises indicated for the future activities of White Eagle and his group of the White Brotherhood, we accepted the position as inevitable and proceeded to make preparations for the opening.

Grace Cooke, in PLUMED SERPENT

The lease was signed on 20 January, and Pembroke Hall, redecorated and furnished, was dedicated and opened, under the name of The White Eagle Lodge, on 22 February 1936. It seems incredible, looking back, when we realise how much was accomplished in those few short weeks, and it is a tribute to Minesta's ever-creative vision that she was able from the start to see not what the place was but what it could be, the friendly and beautiful home for the White Eagle work which the public first saw on that great day. It was a

The main chapel at Pembroke Hall, arranged for a service

tribute also to the devotion and industry of the little group from the time at Burstow who stood firm after the closure and gave unstinted help in this great new venture.

White Eagle has always taught that workers for the spirit had also to be prepared to get down on their knees and scrub the floor of their Lodge, and this we now found ourselves doing. Brother Faithful built the platform, altar and reading desks, with his own hands. As well as the main chapel, there was a small chapel where later all the early 'inner teachings' were to be given.

> The altar, and other furnishings from the Manor House chapel, served to make a smaller chapel, as nearly as possible a replica, and it was remarkable how the power and sanctity of the former chapel seemed to return.
>
> *Ivan Cooke, in* THE WHITE BROTHERHOOD

On the opening day the new chapel, transformed from the somewhat seedy dance-hall, was filled to capacity; and sharing the platform with Minesta and Brother Faithful were Estelle Stead and Shaw Desmond, well-known figures in the Spiritualist Movement. The last-named, with a flash of insight, referred to the Lodge as a lighthouse in the dark world, a theme which White Eagle took up in his address. Later, that symbol of the lighthouse was going to mean a great deal. We quote now from White Eagle's dedication of the Lodge:

> We have chosen to call this centre the White Eagle Lodge – a name not bearing reference to any particular person but referring to the white eagle as a symbol of vision, used down the ages by the Wise Ones whom we are privileged to serve.
>
> This is to be a centre of light; and all who would serve the Great White Light, whatever their denomination, whatever their school of thought, can meet here on a common plane of brother-hood and service.
>
> Therefore, beloved children, we say that this place is to be a lighthouse to guide men, and we ask you to help us establish and maintain the light within. Let this become a focal point for the light of spirit.
>
> Unite with us in spirit so that we may be at one with the Christ Light.
>
> Now we would ask you to be absolutely still within; to put aside all worldly cares and thoughts, to be ready and open and so contact the great Light which is now pouring down upon us all . . .
>
> In the name of God we call upon the Angels of Light, of Wisdom and of Power, to bless, sanctify and dedicate this centre to the service of Christ. May those who minister herein heal the sick and comfort those who mourn; may they remove the blindfold from the eyes of those who see not, and give hearing to those who are deaf; may they at all times give forth from their

hearts and lives the love of God, bringing peace on earth, helping to establish brotherhood between men and harmony between nations.

So be it.

In the words of the Master we say: *Feed my sheep* – in daily service and love.

Pembroke Hall stood at the meeting of five roads, and if you were to go today and stand where the old Lodge stood you might wonder how a quiet work of prayer and communion and spiritual healing and teaching could ever be accomplished or even contemplated there. Well, it was quieter then; not quite the rush and roar of traffic that there is today. But more than this, a seven-foot solid brick wall stood between us and the road (there is still a wall there today) and once through the narrow gate into the little courtyard beyond you were in a new and quieter world. And you would go straight forward through what must at one time have been a small conservatory – for it was all glass – into the main chapel, which seated about a hundred and fifty people and was quiet and peaceful with its blue curtains, white walls and the simple altar adorned with the fragrant *Longii* lilies, the weekly gift of one kind member.

The conservatory (swelteringly hot in summer of course) was an excellent vestibule for the main chapel. On the left was a tiny room not much more than four by five feet, which was Brother Faithful's office. Here he did all his writing in those early days – he was a prolific writer – and from here he would emerge benign and humorous to greet and talk to visitors and take new patients under his wing (for in those very early days he was our chief and only healer). This little room also housed the first White Eagle Lodge library (it must have had expanding walls). On the right of the vestibule was the secretary's office, slightly bigger but not much so, though it was a pleasant little room with a window looking out onto the courtyard and an escape route through the main chapel which the harassed secretary sometimes found very useful!

If you preferred, instead of going forward into the main chapel you could turn left as you entered the courtyard, and walk round the building into a quiet little paved garden sheltering under a plane tree; and from the garden you would pass into a small cottage. Fairly elderly and somewhat cramped it was, but never mind! It served to provide a meeting room and cloakroom for members. Then there was a small kitchen in which the member was greeted by a little old-fashioned lady clad in spotless white apron and wearing high-buttoned boots, who provided tea and delicious thin bread and butter. She was always known as Mrs Button-Boots.

Upstairs was a room of which gracious and lovely memories remain, for this was 'White Eagle's room' where all the early spiritual unfoldment groups took place, the room where the first

Library
A member has presented some thirty books to our Library, thus denuding her own bookshelves to the great advantage of our readers . . . We gratefully acknowledge a valuable gift which will bring profit and help to many.
ANGELUS, April 1938

Brotherhood chapel at Pembroke Hall, arranged for an absent healing group

[The Third Anniversary Service:] For the first time a microphone was installed, and a record taken of practically the entire service. Until she heard these records White Eagle's medium had never before heard his voice - a strange and notable fact, considering that the two have worked together for some thirty years. The set of records also forms a most valuable memento of our third Anniversary.

ANGELUS, March 1939

instruction in meditation was given (it was then a little-known art in the West), and the room to which many a soul came seeking comfort in their grief or need, and so often emerged – radiant and transformed after a private hour with White Eagle. In this room also Minesta had the memorable contact (described in THE SHINING PRESENCE) with the Master from India, which had a profound effect upon her.

This room lay directly above the Members' Room, and it was all the inevitable chatter below that led Brother Faithful to indite his memorable notice to those using the room: 'Please keep your conversation low'! A narrow passage divided this room from the two small healing chapels partitioned off in those few short weeks between the signing of the lease and the opening day: and from this passage a way had been cut through the thick wall to the balcony over the main chapel. It was a very small opening, resulting in many a bruised head. We guessed it was to teach us humility!

We have described Pembroke Hall in some detail, feeling that these early beginnings will be of special interest to all our friends and family. It will be seen how perfectly adapted was this whole building to the then needs of the Lodge, and how true had been White Eagle's guidance in leading us there.

After the opening came the period of building. Looking back on those early days it is difficult to imagine how Minesta and Brother Faithful managed to sustain single-handed, with a secretarial staff of one [Ylana – though with wonderful voluntary help], the programme of activities they set themselves, but both were full of enthusiasm and a burning desire to help humanity, and seemed to be carried along by a spiritual power far greater than their own. They certainly needed it, for as well as two public services each week, there was a weekly Inner Teaching by White Eagle as well as many private appointments for healing, guidance and consolation.

All the public services were conducted by Minesta and Brother Faithful, both of whom were experienced in public work. Minesta was a superb clairvoyant and when the White Eagle Lodge was first opened she would give clairvoyance at all the public meetings except when White Eagle was speaking, for she felt that this was a way of drawing enquirers and support to the Lodge.

Joan Hodgson, 'Personal Recollections of Minesta and White Eagle',
STELLA POLARIS, *June–July 1980*

From small beginnings the work at Pembroke Hall grew and flourished. It was a great act of faith, for its founders had no capital behind them on which to run the Lodge, and were extremely dependent on the goodwill of White Eagle followers and the hard work of those involved. Friends were invited to support the Lodge by becoming Members, and we still remember the very first to walk into the little office and pay her subscription – one guinea then.

Her name was Edith Quinlan, and she became a good friend and faithful worker. It was she who very shortly afterwards introduced to the Lodge the 'grey-haired stranger' who became our first organist. The original number of members was a hundred and twenty, a number which slowly but very surely grew. The goodwill has never been lacking; nor has the faith that if those most closely involved really served and gave from their hearts, all material needs would be met. That faith has always been justified, though it must be confessed that there have been anxious moments!

White Eagle had already spoken at Burstow about a new method of spiritual healing through light rays which was to form an important part of the work in the future. It was shortly after the opening of the Lodge that he directed us to form the absent healing groups which have become such a feature of the White Eagle path. Healers were trained under his guidance, and the new method of the mental and spiritual projection of coloured light rays, in co-operation with the angels of healing, about which we were beginning to learn, got under way. At first there were just two groups, gradually increasing to the five which were working at the time war broke out in 1939.

Another event which had a great effect on the future of the work was the appearance, in duplicated form, of a monthly Lodge magazine – ANGELUS – in response to direct guidance, even as to the name itself, given to Minesta. ANGELUS offered us a chance to keep in touch with our small band of members and to help to draw them together as a family – as STELLA POLARIS does today. The name was to give the feeling of the 'call to prayer'. Soon we read:

The first issue of ANGELUS has been kindly received. Its readers have overlooked shortcomings, praised any merits, and translated their kindliness into action by either passing on their own copy, or obtaining further copies for their friends. ANGELUS and its staff anticipated no less.

Do not, however, enquire of the editorial staff (comprising one person) why the first issue of ANGELUS was duplicated and not printed. Do not stress the many advantages of printing over duplicating. The staff will only respond with a pallid smile. It knows the answer. Do not repeat your question in our duplicating, binding and despatching Works (the Works measuring six feet by eight, and staffed by two persons). They have turned the handle of the duplicator many thousands of times; sorted, arranged and bound so many of the sheets! they know, also – none better. Why rouse them to frenzy, or send them into a decline?

Nevertheless, ANGELUS, made beautiful and more perfect, will, in due course, go out into the world in printed form and thus carry its message to the many instead of the few.

Ivan Cooke in ANGELUS, *July 1936*

You will greatly help the Editorial Staff of ANGELUS if you decide to become a regular subscriber. The annual subscription (eleven issues) is 6/- post free.

ANGELUS, May 1937

The literature and teaching here received has hitherto circulated mostly among those who attend the Lodge. Now it is to seek a wider field. Small beginnings, however; always, as with nature, but a tender shoot is put forth, a bud of life which may become a tree, a forest, may clothe a countryside, or eventually reach across a world. And our particular putting forth will be but the printing of a selection of White Eagle's Addresses in an inexpensive handbook.

ANGELUS, May 1937

THE CHRISTIAN MYSTERIES . . . For weeks and weeks we have pored over proofs from the printers, pondered on and discussed this, that, and the other; settled where this and that illustration shall appear, discussed cover design, weeded out superfluous commas scattered by the printer's largesse . . . Anticipation runs high. We know this to be the best sent forth so far as contents go; the pages will be printed and bound as beautifully and worthily as possible. We have done our best. In the meantime, we are trusting in the powers that be . . . and in our printer.

ANGELUS, November 1938

A promise which was eventually redeemed, as we shall see.

In 1937 we published the first-ever book of White Eagle's teaching, ILLUMINATION. It consisted of talks he gave before the opening of the Lodge, at various Spiritualist services in London. Printed on deckle-edged paper in large type, it was illustrated with woodcuts and bound in stiff board covers and sold for two shillings. We shall never forget the thrill of opening the first batch of books the printers delivered. The smell of the ink lingers, amid many memories of that great moment. How splendid our previously empty bookstall looked once the new books were on display!

ILLUMINATION immediately won new friends to the Lodge, one of whom was none other than our dear John Hodgson. Another whom it brought in that year was a young man who many years later was to become our legal adviser: Noel Gabriel. So we owe that book quite a lot. This period also saw another come into the Lodge whose gifts were to be greatly valued later: Teddy Dent, the author of the two poems reproduced in the book MEDITATION (and the father of Geoffrey Dent).

The first book was followed after six months by another, WAYS OF SERVICE IN THE WORLD TODAY, consisting of inner teachings given in the new Lodge; and later in 1938 came THE CHRISTIAN MYSTERIES, another set of recent inner teachings (interpreting, largely, the Revelation of St John). The newly-formed 'White Eagle Publications' thus succeeded in publishing three books in sixteen months, no mean achievement. These three and ANGELUS, together with the regular distribution of the White Eagle inner teachings in duplicated form, established the White Eagle Lodge in the love and respect of a following which soon extended beyond the shores of this country. We read in ANGELUS, for instance, of 'a large order for copies of ILLUMINATION for New York'. We have happy memories of the great effort each week to transcribe, type, duplicate and assemble copies of the inner teachings ready for sale the week after they were given. Our two gallant helpers in this task are still with us today. One of them, Leonard Willis, Brother 'Steadfast', is still very much involved in the running of the London Lodge and has stood by our side for almost our full fifty years. They used to rush to the Lodge from work in order to help with the assembly and stapling of the pages so that the customer had them 'hot from the press'.

Another whom we remember with very deep affection from this period is our organist, Reginald Botcherby, who became Brother 'John': the 'grey-haired stranger'.

When he first came the Lodge had been opened for just four weeks and White Eagle was appealing for the beautiful music which he said was essential to the work. By the end of April our grey-haired stranger was playing the organ at a Sunday service and he was subsequently to transform the musical scene which he had found . . . Probably few realise with what care he built the musical structure of the services so that there should be no jarring note . . . We must refer to his work with the choir which he formed – a prolonged but triumphant struggle against a dearth of tenors and basses, against black-out and bombs.

Obituary, ANGELUS, *March 1945*

*

Anyone who examines the early publications will see that they were available not only from Pembroke Hall but also from 'the Scottish branch of the Lodge', 8 Rosebery Crescent, Edinburgh. This 'branch' was to play an important part in the Lodge history, but its beginnings are even more remarkable.

It was just a few months after the English group of the Brotherhood formed that it began. The group's leader, 'David' Burn-Callander, had just returned from Fanning Island, in the remote Pacific, when he first met Minesta. On the island he had received a message through another's mediumship. Minesta writes:

The message purported to come from a spirit, who said he was working to establish groups of White Brothers on the earth. The spirit went on to say that [Major Burn-Callander] would leave Fanning Island and return to Edinburgh; there he would meet a certain Mrs Cooke, through whom he would be guided to his future work in connection with a Brotherhood. Up to this point [he] had not heard my name and quite simply asked me if I had ever come across a Mrs. Cooke in the course of my travels. To our mutual amusement, I confessed that my name happened to be Cooke.   *Grace Cooke, in* PLUMED SERPENT

Later White Eagle spoke to the young man through Minesta and told him, as further confirmation, the name under which he had manifested on Fanning Island. The Edinburgh group thus began under White Eagle's clearest instructions.

By 1938 there were eighteen initiated brothers in Edinburgh, and the work of absent and contact healing as well as the Brotherhood work for peace closely mirrored that of the Lodge in London. In July 1939 an announcement in ANGELUS stated:

For about five years there has been a branch of the Brotherhood in [Edinburgh], which for some time past has been outgrowing its premises. The opening of a White Eagle Lodge to house the Brotherhood in Edinburgh is therefore a logical outcome.

A date was set for it, 6 October.

In the event things did not quite work out as planned. As the September ANGELUS went to press, war broke out. Yet the opening of the Edinburgh Lodge, when it did come, was to play a vital part in the Lodge story.

2

The War Years

WHEN WAR came, it was the dashing of many, many hopes and the seeming frustration of months, indeed years, of work for the Light, for peace, by the Brotherhood. More than this, it appeared to call White Eagle's authority into question, for he had said repeatedly that he did not foresee war. For instance, in a remarkable interview with the editor of PSYCHIC NEWS given in 1938 just before Neville Chamberlain despatched the telegram to Hitler which resulted in their Munich meeting, he said:

> I foresee a period of peace . . . I do not think there will be a war. I think the war clouds will pass away. But mankind is passing through a tremendous struggle, not only on earth but on the spiritual planes of his being. There are two forces at work, the destructive and the constructive. If man persists in his fears, he is helping to bring about the very thing that he fears.
>
> THE WHITE BROTHERHOOD

In his prophecy White Eagle was not alone: his brother guides in the Spiritualist movement and in occultism said just the same, then and after. A year later it was difficult to comprehend how they could have prophesied peace. War was declared on 3 September 1939, and it seemed to discredit what the guides had said. White Eagle acknowledged this in a talk a week later:

> There has been a great question among Spiritualists as to why the message that there will be no war was given through so many mediums, through so many occult channels. The message was decreed by the Great Lords . . . We in the beyond do not question those in a higher position . . . Man's criticism and condemnation, if our work proved an apparent failure, was not our concern. Our one aim was to help to keep hope alive in as many hearts as possible for once hope had died the channel for spiritual light and power became closed.
>
> Fear is the weak spot in us all, and this fear abiding in the hearts of humanity had to be counteracted, even to the last possible moment . . . Without confidence and hope the Forces of Light could no longer hold the fort against the enemy . . .
>
> There will be a sudden cessation of hostilities. God is omnipotent. So far and no farther can man go. Man's freewill is encompassed by the will of God, and God's hand will be stretched forth at the appointed hour, when lessons have been learnt, and 'halt' will be called . . .
>
> We see joy and rejoicing, we see a glorious peace as the outcome, a rapid growth of brotherhood on earth. Already the brotherhood is being born. Birth pangs must always be painful.

God will not test you beyond your strength and even through these troublous days you will find compensation.

White Eagle's address on 10 September 1939,
reprinted in ANGELUS, *October 1939*

Men and women who lived through the years before the declaration of war will remember how fear and anticipation built up as the various European crises came and went. During this whole period White Eagle, in company with other spiritual teachers, constantly encouraged his followers to think positively: to hold the thought that there would be no war; to radiate light to balance and dissipate the forces of darkness which were massing for the great conflict, the 'years of fire' predicted by the White Brotherhood in spirit. During the crisis in 1938 Brotherhood groups in the Lodge had been meeting every three hours to work on the inner planes for peace. The intensity of the work comes across clearly in the book THE WHITE BROTHERHOOD, completed just at the moment war was declared. We recall clearly the continual effort to hold fast to the thought of the Star, radiating light and peace; and to remain steady and peaceful. It was not easy, because one was fighting natural personal fears of the unknown, and constantly being battered by the radio news bulletins and the dire headlines which shouted from every newspaper.

> The outbreak of war in September 1939 dealt a shattering blow to the ordered lives of those who worked at, or regularly worshipped in, the Lodge . . . Spiritual truths and spiritual wisdom appeared to be at a discount. All the prophecies of the spirit guides had apparently proved failures; for here we were, plunged into war and entering one of the darkest periods in the dreadful history of war . . .
>
> On the outer plane it seemed a challenge from the forces of materialism to the forces of Light. On the inner, I felt that the spiritual structure of the Lodge was assailed by the enormous waves of materialism and pessimism. The work stood fast, however, unshaken in its purpose – a purpose which with the passing days seemed more and more essential, for without the Lodge many of our followers would have been bereft indeed. Here it is interesting to note that one with clairvoyant vision had seen the Lodge as an oasis of light in a spiritually darkened city.
>
> *Grace Cooke, in* PLUMED SERPENT

Blue is the pervading colour of the White Eagle Lodge. The altar is of blue, set against a background of natural (unstained) oak. From above this background a row of shaded blue lighting falls on the plain oaken cross, the lilies and burning candles; while above the lighting is the life-size carving of a white eagle in flight – a graceful and beneficent figure.

ANGELUS, March 1939

In retrospect, then, it is remarkable how unshaken the Lodge was by the apparent counteraction of the 'no-war prophecies'; and this in turn is an indication of how far White Eagle's following understood the deeper meaning and purpose of his work, rather than the literal words. This must partly be because White Eagle himself stood so firm, as his words on 10 September 1939 indicate. In fact, some of White Eagle's most important teaching was given during these years; and he guided the Brotherhood's work with remarkable detail all through the period of conflict, on many occasions showing extraordinary knowledge of future events. The Brotherhood was formed to help humanity through 'the years of fire', and so when these years came, the brothers knew their work and they continued with it.

But as most readers know, the declaration of war, was followed by what became known as the 'phoney' war, when nothing much seemed to be happening.

> After those first few weeks of chaos, the work of the Lodge returned close to normal except that the black-out made late evening services impossible, and during the war years the Sunday services in winter were always held in the afternoons. Following the instructions of White Eagle, the devoted band of workers who remained still strove to maintain the Lodge as a centre of peace, love and brotherhood, a place set apart from the fevers of war. The spiritual light was sent forth into the warring world at every third hour of the day.
>
> *Joan Hodgson and Ylana Hayward,*
> *in* BY WHAT AUTHORITY? (1953)

TO OUR READERS. – Owing to the shortage of paper, we have been obliged to make use of smaller type for this and future subsequent issues of ANGELUS, and thus, without curtailing the contents, reduce the number of pages for each issue. We hope our readers will think we have chosen the lesser of two disagreeable alternatives.

ANGELUS, May 1940

The book THE WHITE BROTHERHOOD was published in November 1939, held up for a couple of months by the declaration of war. It had been written to draw more workers into the chains for peace, and thus its publication, when war had been declared, was an act of courage. Yet it was needed more than ever.

*

In the November ANGELUS that year the editor proudly proclaimed: 'Beginning with the December issue, the Christmas number, our journal will be printed'. And he was able to write in January 1940: 'The reception given to the Christmas ANGELUS has been extraordinarily kind – but this we never doubted . . . We do ask our readers to add their efforts to ours by passing on their copy of ANGELUS and so cooperating with us . . . The blacker the blackout the greater the need for spiritual illumination in these days.' Later we read that the Christmas issue fell short of the requirements by some hundreds of copies – so it can be seen that the printed ANGELUS got off to a good start and never looked back.

Thus was redeemed the promise to which we referred earlier. Three months later, in March 1940, another hope was realised, for the Edinburgh Lodge was indeed opened and dedicated by White Eagle on the 30th of that month – an event reported and described by no less august a voice than that of THE SCOTSMAN.

In July 1940, just before the onset of the blitz, came a stirring call to service from White Eagle, in an address subsequently entitled 'Let there be Light'. In the course of the address he spoke of

The main chapel of the Edinburgh Lodge at 98 Hanover Street

'principalities and powers' and of 'darkness in high places', of the balance between the forces of light and darkness, and of our responsibility and power to help, of how the advance of darkness could be halted by the light.

The 'Cross of Light' poster

> By adopting a positive attitude, by recognising only the power of the Divine Spirit, and by breathing into your being, morning, noon and night, the Spirit of Christ; by visualising in the mind of your heart the perfect, the gentle, the divine Man, you will create in your aura a light sufficient to reinforce your weaker brethren . . .
>
> Think, my brethren, what the effect would be if millions in your country were thus radiating light! Think what the effect would be if men abandoned thoughts of self, desire for accumulation or protection for self, and held fast to one dominating thought of peace and brotherhood, and to help men to the way of Christ! Will you make this effort? For we tell you that the hosts of heaven are ready and waiting to help man.
>
> This spirit of the Light of Christ will save mankind, and this spirit alone . . .
>
> We pray that everyone hearing our words will be touched, and make a supreme effort, and . . . become receptive to the Divine Light of Christ! Send it forth again and again, so that your country, this mystic isle, shall appear in the etheric world as a blazing Cross of Light which no power of darkness can harm . . .
>
> Were a picture of the Cross of Light displayed on many buildings, in many places . . . the continual beholding of such a sign of power would create a ring of defence around this isle. May this Cross become a living symbol, cleansing the nation of hatred or desire for vengeance, protecting and saving the people . . . Your work must not be stayed for one instant. Put on the whole armour of God. Be filled with the power of the Spirit of Christ . . . Go forward in this spiritual battle.
>
> *Address of 7 July 1940, reprinted as a leaflet*

It was as a direct result of this message from White Eagle that the famous 'Cross of Light' poster campaign was launched. Let Minesta herself describe it.

> A message was received from the beyond that the White Brotherhood wished to have a special poster printed, showing a sleeping city, and above, in the night sky, a large illumined cross with rays of light from it radiating a protective influence over the city . . . The circle of light was symbolic of the universal power of God, the rose on the cross signified the potential love of Christ in the hearts of men . . .
>
> The designing and preparation of this poster occupied some weeks, it being completed early in August 1940. It will be noted how accurately the beyond anticipated the arrival of the blitzkrieg. Each poster was blessed before being sent out. In other words, in a Brotherhood group the spiritual light was focused upon the

posters so that henceforth they became centres of spiritual power. Many thousands of these posters were distributed. They were to be seen, during the worst months of the bombardment suffered by London, on every Underground and Tube station (in which many thousands of people nightly took shelter), displayed on hoardings, on church doors, in factories and in shops all over England and Scotland . . .

Grace Cooke, in PLUMED SERPENT

The posters are remembered today by persons who knew nothing of the Lodge but found protection and strength from them. We had many letters from people relating how many houses displaying the posters had been undamaged when neighbouring buildings had taken the full force of bomb blast. One woman wrote to say that, carrying the poster, she was untouched by a bomb which fell only a few feet away. Perhaps more important than this, however, was the power the displayed poster had of focusing the forces of Light, of lifting people above the level of fear. As the Battle of Britain reached its height at the beginning of September 1940, the control of the cloud of fear must have been very important to those in the beyond who were working to save humanity. The poster was also a great source of strength to all of us in the Lodge, as we shall see.

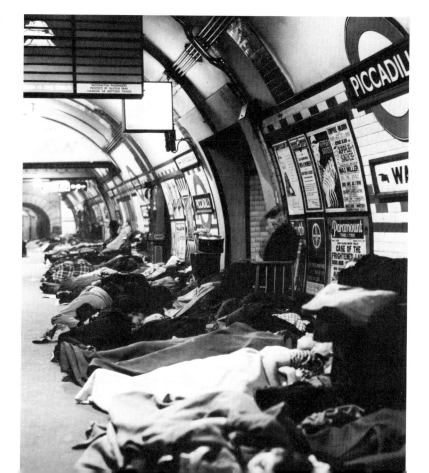

Piccadilly Tube Station, during an air raid in 1940. Note the 'Cross of Light' poster to the right of the seated man.

*

The first Sunday in September was the opening of the Autumn Session. White Eagle gave the address and concluded by making a most unusual request. He said that the Wise Ones requested us to prepare for a special Service of Communion on the following Sunday. Such a Service had never been held before in the Lodge. Arrangements previously made as to speakers, etc., had to be cancelled . . .

Those who attended this Service of Communion are little likely to forget it . . .

At the conclusion of the Sacrament [received, as in Lodge services today, in meditation], White Eagle stepped from the rostrum and walked down the aisle for the whole length of the hall, blessing all in the assembly. When he returned to the platform he uttered the last words he ever spoke in that hall.

Grace Cooke, PLUMED SERPENT

Woodcut by 'Swoz' (F.E.Swarsbrick) from the early publications

These were the closing words:

In the Name of our Lord and King Who is the Christ, we pray . . . *Father, forgive them, for they know not what they do* . . .

May the peace of the Holy Spirit bless you and keep you safe in His love, now and always. Amen.

And now, the angels will minister to you. Christ's Angels will minister to each one of you; and you may likewise minister on earth to your fellow men in the days to come.

ANGELUS, October 1940

That service was on Sunday 8 September. On the night of Thursday 12 September Pembroke Hall was hit by a bomb and was destroyed.

We may be permitted to dwell on some personal recollections at this point. Joan (Hodgson), who had continued her job as a schoolteacher in the first twelve months of the War and had been evacuated to the country, recalls:

'After the first panic at the outbreak of war was over I had been drafted back to London, and at first had to walk round the streets gathering groups of children together and trying to find places where we could give them some lessons and keep them out of mischief. Gradually the empty schools had reopened, not in their old form but with an odd selection of staff who returned from being evacuated; and somehow we all worked together under the guidance of the most senior member. Thus it was that at the time when the blitz started I found myself teaching in a school near Barnes Common. And whenever the air-raid siren went we trooped out with all the children into prepared trenches on the common.

'It was after one of those afternoons spent with the children in a trench that the rest of the family picked me up for the journey back to Kent after they had discovered Pembroke Hall in ruins. Although they were full of this dire news, they were unable to pour out the

Woodcut by 'Swoz' (F.E.Swarsbrick) from the early publications

story because we were giving a lift to one of my colleagues!'

Ylana writes: 'I remember the extraordinary calm which seemed to grip us when to the sound of wailing sirens announcing yet another raid we arrived to find Pembroke Hall in ruins. Perhaps it was just that it didn't register. I think what really brought us down to earth was when the florist arrived with the usual lilies for the altar for the next Sunday service. It was rather like laying a wreath on the grave!'.

The remarkable thing, of course, is that no-one was inside the building when it was demolished.

> One of our members – as a rule unable to attend the Lodge on a Sunday – had an urge to come to that special Service of Communion. She said about herself and her husband: 'I really cannot account for the feeling, but I felt we simply *had* to come.' After the Service was over, and the congregation was dispersing, this friend came to me and said: 'I have just thought that you and your family might come home with us tonight. It will mean fresh country air and perhaps a good night's rest. Will you come? I hesitated for a few moments; then I heard White Eagle's voice saying: 'Go; yes, go.'
>
> *Grace Cooke, in* PLUMED SERPENT

White Eagle later instructed the family to stay in the country for a few more days, and thus it was that on the night of 12 September, the night the bomb fell, they were not sleeping in the Lodge as they had been doing, feeling safer there than in their London flat.

The news was given to our members in words which even today we find moving. We quote from the October ANGELUS.

> Our readers will learn with sorrow and regret that Pembroke Hall, which has housed the London Lodge for some four years, was partially demolished one night by a bomb which fell nearby . . . Those who have worshipped in the Lodge will grieve with us. The peace and beauty which it enshrined would seem destroyed almost beyond redemption, the work built up with such loving care wantonly shattered.
>
> The above is a first reaction; deeper lies the realisation that the work of the White Eagle Lodge still dwells in the hearts of men; that one supremely loving heart can still lead and help men . . . The White Eagle Lodge is founded in this love and brotherhood, and, we believe, must go forward. What has happened to the building which housed the Lodge cannot destroy the work done. Rather it is an incentive to greater effort in the future, even as humanity has now greater need for such work than ever before . . .
>
> As to the future we have high hearts. We shall seek new premises, and a greater and more beautiful White Eagle Lodge will arise from what has been razed.
>
> *Ivan Cooke, in* ANGELUS, *October 1940*

The magazine went on to print the words of the last Communion Service.

Though the family had been remarkably preserved, and much of the furniture had escaped serious damage, the building had not. Why had it been allowed to happen? was a very human question to ask. White Eagle said: 'You must share the fate of humanity if you would learn to give true help and understanding in such a time of need. Why should you escape the common lot?'

> And, in parting, we trust that faithful brethren will learn not to take too much notice of apparent earthly disasters. Take all changes philosophically and see in them a means to a finer end. Nothing is really disastrous; it is only when the vision is limited that disaster is seen. When the vision extends into the great beyond, the soul sees a Light, and love and wisdom and beauty. You are not left alone. Remember the silent Brethren by your side, they will never forsake you. There is nothing to fear in life – except the enemy of all mankind, which is fear. Overcome this last enemy, and you will have found the secret way into heaven.
>
> *White Eagle, in* ANGELUS, *October 1940*

So far as Minesta was concerned, the bigger the catastrophe, the greater the courage, and within a few days of the bombing the search was on for new premises. Joan took compassionate leave from her teaching job, and the day after she left it they set forth through the air raids to visit possible buildings. They were led to St Mary Abbots Place, only a quarter of a mile from the old Lodge. On entering what is now the main chapel, Minesta said: 'This is the place. I shall work here'. And she did!

During the months following the bombing the extraordinary provision of those in the inner world who hold the overall plan of the work became apparent. The new White Eagle Lodge in Edinburgh dedicated by White Eagle in the previous spring became home for the work. While negotiations were in hand for the new London building, we were invited by our Scottish friends and brothers to make our home with them until Christmas (or until negotiations were completed). This meant that the spiritual work could continue without a break: Sunday services, healing and unfoldment groups, and inner teachings. The publication of ANGELUS continued, though Brother Faithful was to complain gently in its pages: 'The secretarial work of the Lodge (which includes the preparation of this journal) is done partly in Kent, partly in Hampshire and in part in Edinburgh, a factor making neither for efficiency nor convenience'. He added, 'It is a grief also that we cannot have our Annual Christmas Tree at Pembroke Hall, a joyful episode to which we have usually looked forward at this Season'. He needn't have worried! For a most joyous Christmas service was held in the Edinburgh Lodge, and he later wrote: 'At one corner of the Lodge stood a laden Christmas

LODGE ACTIVITIES.– We hope that our readers will not think of the work of the London Lodge as finished, or even suspended. We rather believe that the spiritual powers which centred their power on the Lodge are more active than ever.

ANGELUS, November 1940

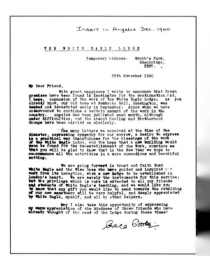

Minesta's letter of 25 November 1940 announcing that new premises had been found for the Lodge.

The annual Christmas Tree, with presents for needy children (1938)

The main chapel of the Lodge at St Mary Abbots Place in the days of the School for Animal Painting, for whom the building was constructed in 1911/12

tree, and a congregation outflowed into an adjoining room. In spirit, atmosphere, and joy it was like a Christmas service at Pembroke Hall . . . those Christmas services of happy memories'.

It was as a result of the difficult circumstances that the possibility of 'lone healing' work became apparent. As soon as it was known that we were functioning from Edinburgh, people began to write for healing. To cope with this need healers with experience in the London Lodge were asked to co-operate by doing their work in their own homes at the normal time of the healing group. All the sitters had a copy of the service and a list of patients. Sometimes several would meet together in someone's home, otherwise they would tune in on their own; and somehow we coped with the growing list of patients. As Joan had just come into the work and had no specific responsibility, it seemed natural that she should take over the organisation of this healing work. (This development, which was outwardly due to force of circumstances, fulfilled a prophecy which White Eagle had made to her in the Burstow days when she was anxious about finding the right teaching post. He said: 'Your guide is watching over you all the time and will not allow you to miss the right opportunity when it comes. You will find yourself teaching children of all ages'.)

Back now to London and the new Lodge! And in January 1941 Brother Faithful prepared readers of ANGELUS for the opening:

We have a new home for a new age, new work to undertake. When you enter our new Lodge (as we hope you will and soon) you may think that here is a simple yet gracious (and spacious) building. For what purpose it was originally built we do not know – an art school, perhaps, or a studio accommodating many students [this was a right assumption]. The building is situated in a quiet *cul de sac* off the Kensington High Street, known as St Mary Abbots Place, from which a door opens to a paved court, across which an entrance flanked on either side by pillars admits one to the main hall, a portion of which is raised as for a stage (here can be presented the mystical plays we have planned, and even commenced to produce last year). The hall has walls of white, a floor covered with white rubber, concealed lighting and central heating [hardly 'central' or even 'heating' by modern standards!] and will seat rather more people than Pembroke Hall – considerably more if the balcony overhead be used . . .

We hope the foregoing gives no wrong impression of grandiloquence or lavishness. All is simple, yet with a simplicity akin to graciousness that will become beauty when the chapel is furnished and endowed with spiritual power.

When furnished! Alas, the furnishings from the Hall are dusty, shabby, scarred, the curtains and carpets deeply impregnated – as is everything else – with a pulverised mortar dust, adhesive almost beyond belief. A formidable task opens. No

mere dusting or banging will suffice, but a wholehearted scrubbing, perhaps in many waters, will be called for. So far as possible we shall retain and repair our furnishings, partly for association's sake, partly because battle scars are honourable. But our organ lies in matchwood back in the shambles which was Pembroke Hall, with many another article smashed beyond redemption . . .
But think of the thrill of making ready, of reconstruction!

ANGELUS, *January 1941*

Two of the willing team who put their backs into this 'formidable task' (our editor did not exaggerate) were the Brameld twins, Mary and Elizabeth. They were only children then, still at school; but with their mother (Sister 'Hope', later to become a pillar of service in the Lodge), they scrubbed and cleaned and polished with a will.

We mention them particularly because a few years later Mary was called by White Eagle to fill the place at the organ left empty (except for a few more temporary helpers) when Brother 'John' died early in 1945. This she continued to do through the 1950s and 1960s, and indeed still regularly takes her place at the organ of the London Lodge, though it is a much more sophisticated instrument now than the small Positive organ (shown in the photograph on page 39) – one manual, four stops and no pedals, but dear to our hearts – which replaced the one destroyed in Pembroke Hall.

And so, after much hard but happy work, the new home for White Eagle's work was opened and dedicated by him on Saturday, 22 March, at three o'clock, and thus began a whole new era in the story of the White Eagle Lodge.

In the course of his talk at the dedication White Eagle said: 'I tell you that if this temple be cast down tomorrow, it will be rebuilt again, and rebuilt again and yet again; for this is the law of the Cosmos, making for resurrection and life eternal'.

Thanks be to God, we were not called upon to put White Eagle's words to the test – although we did almost immediately have three fire-bombs descend on the roof of the Lodge. They miraculously burnt themselves out. Another fell in 1943, when an unknown hero rushed in from the street and volunteered to go up into the roof, where he put out the fire blazing there. He then disappeared as anonymously as he had come.

Quietly and steadily, and in spite of the difficulties, dangers and restrictions of wartime, the work grew and developed both on the outer plane and in inner strength. It was a period of rebuilding and consolidation. In the ANGELUS of October 1941 the six Principles of the Lodge, formulated under White Eagle's guidance, were printed for the first time, together with an interpretation of the Lodge symbol of the cross of Light within the circle of Light with the star at its centre. The formulation of these principles seemed to establish the independent being of the Lodge and, looking back, they

A Letter.
My Dear Friends,
At the end of our term of work in Edinburgh we returned south to find a large batch of packets, letters, and Christmas cards awaiting us. We have been so deeply touched by the many messages of kindliness and goodwill that I must beg a space in ANGELUS through which to tell you what happiness your Christmas greetings brought.
Grace Cooke, in ANGELUS, January 1941

The main altar at St Mary Abbots Place (1950 or earlier)

THE LEAFLETS. If we cannot publish books at least we can print leaflets. Readers will find a list of those already published in this issue, and perhaps note yet another new leaflet, called, 'PEACE AT HEART'. This is White Eagle's Palm Sunday Address, published in last month's ANGELUS. We hope that you will assist us in the distribution of these leaflets. They are like seeds, and while some will doubtless fall on shallow ground – on careless, indifferent or incredulous soil – some will find a rich and receptive seed bed, and bear a good harvest.

ANGELUS, June 1941

The healing chapels created in 1943

strengthened the work at the inner level – perhaps they would be better described as giving us a foundation on which to work.

1943 was a specially notable year. In April the Lodge was approved for the solemnisation of marriages, and in November the first entry was made in our registers – Joan's marriage to John Hodgson. (We little knew then what a cornerstone of the Lodge John, who was still serving in the R.A.F. at the time, was to become – but no doubt White Eagle did!)

We were now beginning to find that our premises at No. 9 were hardly big enough to contain the expanding work, and therefore were thankful when in the autumn the owners, who also owned the adjoining house, No. 9a, agreed to allow us to include the latter in our agreement at a rental we could just manage. We were able, by making a door between the two buildings, to add another large sanctuary, the present Brotherhood Chapel, which, once the threat of bombings was past, became the permanent place for the inner teachings, the meditation groups and of course the Brotherhood itself. 9a also gave us living accommodation which released room in the main Lodge for a row of little healing chapels, quieter than the old ones, which had been situated on the balcony, where healers and patients were often disturbed by noise and conversation.

The new chapels were dedicated in the autumn at a service attended by fifty people, chiefly Lodge healers. White Eagle said, in his dedication: 'Let nothing be too much trouble when you are dealing with the heart and soul of your brother man. Be tender, considerate and patient – for we are all children of God, who is patient and tender with us all . . . ' We called the healing chapels the Mary Chapel, the Joseph, the Sara Burdett and the Christopher; and they were partitions of the room, outside the new Brotherhood chapel, which now comprises simply the Minesta chapel. At the far end was a Grace Chapel for private prayer and meditation.

'Why the Sara Burdett chapel?', some readers may ask.

Some years ago, before the White Eagle Lodge came into being, and when White Eagle was speaking at various centres and churches in London, one of his most faithful adherents was a certain lady dignified of presence, with a clear, bright colour, and beautiful silver hair. Once White Eagle asked her if she had ever been associated with Annie Besant. She replied in the affirmative. After this incident we came to know her a little better, and discovered that she had been a personal friend and secretary of 'A.B.' . . . The passing of 'A.B.' had brought this phase of our new friend's activities to a close.

When the opening of the White Eagle Lodge was planned, and when premises were found, one of the first to offer her services was Miss Burdett – 'Sara', as she became generally and affectionately known in the Lodge . . . Those who worshipped in Pembroke Hall . . . will recall a figure, tall and upright, and white of hair, seated in the front row of chairs with a note-book and pencil, intent and businesslike.

Ivan Cooke, in ANGELUS, *June 1942*

As well as 'taking down' White Eagle's messages, Sara had brought qualities to the work which were truly manifold: ability in administration, all the experience of her association with the leaders of the Theosophical Society, and wise advice and unfailing support. She worked hard getting the organisation of the healing onto a sound footing and she was a first rate healer herself. She died in 1941, broken as much by the War as by age.

A Thanksgiving Service had been held for her in the Lodge; and for John Hodgson it had been one of the earliest meetings there he attended. He writes, 'It was my first experience of a thanksgiving service, as opposed to the orthodox, sad memorial services which I had attended in my youth. I was struck by the dignity of the presentation, lack of gloom, with the thanksgiving for a life of faithful service the keynote throughout. Most impressive, it was a big step forward on my journey'.

To return to 1943. That year Alison Innes, who has given so many people their first welcome as they entered the Lodge, first came to work here, originally part-time, to help Joan with the healing and astrological work the latter just developing in the Lodge, and then two years later as a full-time worker in the Lodge team, which she continues to be today.

In the meantime things had not been entirely quiet on the publishing front. In November 1943 came the first White Eagle Calendar. It is intriguing to read in ANGELUS, 'Permission from the Ministry of Supply had to be obtained before our Calendar could be printed, a protracted process'!

In addition, between June 1942 and October 1944 all four volumes of the first SPIRITUAL UNFOLDMENT books were published, roughly a book every six months. Also published during the period was Joan's WISDOM IN THE STARS and what was then called PRAYERS OF THE NEW AGE (a title since slightly changed, since the book has been revised and much enlarged).

Despite the expansion of the Lodge work implied in our memories of these years, they were difficult times – as anyone who lived through them will remember. There were the black-out, the air-raids and the flying bombs; the food shortages and restrictions of all kinds; the ever-present scenes of destruction, the depressing newspaper headlines. It is amazing to us that not only was Minesta able to continue her spiritual work in these conditions, but that some very wonderful and sustaining teaching was given during those years of strain and stress. During the worst periods of danger and through the winter months all services were held during daylight hours. We remember one inner teaching given in what is

Sara Burdett

It is anticipated that Mrs Grace Cooke's new book, 'PLUMED SERPENT' (printed by Riders) will be available early in April. The price will be eight shillings and sixpence. Did we mention that the book is illustrated, a factor which, together with war-time costs of production, makes for an increase in the price?

ANGELUS, April 1942

OUR BROTHER THE SUN
Many years ago, we were told by White Eagle that one of the media through which his teaching could be expressed would be music and drama. In pursuance of this guidance the play, 'Our Brother the Sun', was produced to mark the seventh Anniversary of the Lodge.

ANGELUS, April 1943

now the Grace Chapel (but a larger room, altered since to give the present vestibule) when, as we sat listening to White Eagle's loving words, there was a large thud close by and the earth shook as a V-2 landed not far away. White Eagle remained unmoved and we all felt safe and enfolded in angels' wings. Ylana writes, 'There was another occasion when Joan and I, having sought shelter under our office desk during one of the worst night raids, were inexpressibly comforted by the awareness (which came to each of us independently) of being sheltered by great white wings, and we knew that White Eagle was with us and all was well'. These were the sort of experiences which sustained White Eagle's wider family too, along with the unceasing reassurance of his teaching. Here, for instance, is a benediction from a wartime service:

And now, peace be in your hearts . . . peace . . . and know that our love shines as the Sun, giving you all that you need, day by day. That is it! . . . one day at a time . . . day by day. God is in His Heaven; all is well!

ANGELUS, *February 1942*

ENFORCED INTERLUDE. London has been having a disturbing time, as everyone knows. Kensington has not escaped its share of trouble and suffering due to the flying bombs. As a result, the White Eagle Lodge was perforce closed for the latter part of July and it was hoped to re-open on August 13th . . . These lines are written early in August, and at the moment it is impossible to give an exact date for resumption of services and meetings. The chapels at the Lodge, being so largely roofed with glass, are quite unsuitable for public gatherings at the present time.

ANGELUS, September 1944

When V.E. Day came at last, on 8 May 1945, it was celebrated by the happiest of impromptu parties; blackout was torn down, the sandbags removed from the courtyard, and we all turned our faces hopefully to the sun. Later, the War ended in the Far East in the way White Eagle had described in his talk on 10 September 1939.

Despite the crises of 1939 and 1940, the Lodge had come through the War, and had come through it having found an identity, and with the discovery of the value of working together. It had gained, out of an apparent disaster, premises placed right beside one of London's main streets, but where visitors can almost forget they are in London – where the loudest sound is often the birdsong from the neighbouring gardens. Despite the danger from air-raids and the inconvenience of the blackout the Brotherhood's work had continued almost without a break, with brothers attending unfailingly throughout the War; and by some miraculous act of preservation no-one engaged on their Lodge business ever came to harm through enemy action (as, indeed, White Eagle had foretold). Throughout the War all those members engaged on active service were held in the protection of the cross of Light within the circle of Light by groups specially formed for this purpose, and many of those on active service subsequently had remarkable stories to tell of how they were helped, protected and guided. One of these was related to the Brotherhood in May 1940 by the officer himself. After the collapse of the French armies his brigade was surrounded by the enemy and likely to be annihilated. He drew upon the protective power of the Light, which he knew was being given to him by those in the unseen. Miraculously, the brigade was guided

THE CHRISTMAS TREE . . . The Christmas Tree is still standing beside the altar in the Lodge, gaily lit and decorated, and with many presents of toys and woollies about its base. This thing of brightness, human kindness and affection might well symbolise that New Age towards which we all move. Soon the gifts will go away to a North London school for distribution among the very poor children . . . This year we have had 779 toys and woollies given, and the sum of £80 in money, which seems to us a wonderful record.

ANGELUS, January 1945

out of danger and escaped at Dunkirk. The brigadier was our Brother 'Peter', James Hamilton, who was to bring spiritual strength and the power of example to the Lodge for many more years.

The Brotherhood work throughout the war was under very clear and direct guidance from White Eagle and we do believe, humbly, that the Brotherhood made a very real contribution to the victory of the forces of Light during the 'years of fire': the work for which the Brotherhood had been called together in the early 1930s. In moments of great crisis on the battlefield, or in the air or at sea, White Eagle told us, many through their sacrifice or their fulfilment of duty touch the spiritual forces and receive illumination. They make 'contact with this supreme Light; and *you* can help them on the inner or spiritual planes, perhaps more effectively than can thousands on the material plane' (THE BROTHERHOOD TEACHING).

The Lodge had survived the War and it had also grown. The first Daughter Lodge was followed in 1942 by a second Scottish one, in Glasgow. The membership of the whole Lodge had grown, too, from the initial hundred and twenty to about three hundred at the end of the War. Moreover the brothers and closer members of the Lodge had worked together through great trials for up to ten years (in a few cases longer). Even those who lived many miles from the Lodge were linked to the centre by ANGELUS, which had proved a spiritual lifeline to so many during the war years. This was particularly true of the period between the destruction of the first Lodge and the opening of the new premises, when it was our one link (on the outer plane) with our friends and members. Only recently one of our friends described to us how eagerly she awaited the magazine each month, throughout the War. The regular messages from White Eagle in ANGELUS were much looked forward to (particularly as there were fewer White Eagle books available), interspersed as they were with the homely and human remarks of the magazine's editor, Ivan Cooke. Now the Lodge entered a new period, found a new focus to which the effort of the members and brothers could be turned after the very concentrated work which the War had demanded.

THE PURPOSE AND WORK OF THE WHITE EAGLE LODGE. This little booklet has been somewhat delayed, but should be available by the end of February. We hope that all our readers will expend a modest twopence (which is its cost) and read its very interesting contents.

ANGELUS, March 1944

3

New Lands

An early picture of the front entrance to New Lands

ON 24 FEBRUARY 1936, two days after the opening of the Lodge, White Eagle had said: 'We wish you to hold in the invisible the vision of that home in the country, which some day will come into being in spite of all the difficulties and obstacles. Be patient. Never doubt, but hold the vision of this centre, this home in the country . . . It will be the inner mystical centre'. Eight years later, on New Year's Eve, 1944, speaking privately to the family at their little cottage at Headley Down, Hampshire, he left them in no doubt that the time had come to look for this home, to which he had referred at intervals throughout the years since leaving Burstow. He said, 'The place will be found by the Brotherhood invisible . . . it will lie between here and the ancient city of Winchester, it will lie on high ground, and it will be sheltered and screened from cold winds by a belt of trees. It will look out to the view of the setting sun, and on the other side a view of the rising sun. There will be pasture land and orchard; a sweet herb garden and a rose garden. Flowers and flowering shrubs will be there and it will be a place where the Brotherhood of old have tilled the soil . . . It is a fair place with a fair name. In the course of 1945, you will be guided to find it'.

After giving some further detailed description of the property White Eagle added: 'A community of service will be established there . . . Brothers will come to it for quiet and refreshment and training; but the primary purpose is . . . to establish a centre of power, a centre from which will ray forth, not only in your day, but for long, long time after this incarnation has passed, rays of light and power which will eventually bring the whole of Britain under its influence. It is a work with a small beginning, but a vast future.' (1966 Newsletter.)

And so it was that we began looking for the property in the final months of the war. In the second half of April 1945, returning from inspecting a property in the centre of Hampshire, an unplanned diversion was made to another house which was on the market, at Rake, near Petersfield in the same county. The aspect and the setting, the name of the house and the locality, fitted what White Eagle had said exactly.

We shall always remember that first sight of New Lands, standing warm and friendly on the hilltop, in the evening sun. We did not have an order to view but were allowed to walk round the garden. It was a mass of wild daffodils.

And so, against all the advice of the experts and with the help of

A GRANDDAUGHTER FOR MRS. COOKE. We have great pleasure in announcing that on Friday, June 22nd (the time of the Summer Solstice), Mr. and Mrs. Hodgson (née Joan Cooke) were blessed with the heavenly gift of a daughter, Rosemary Grace. The little girl and her mother are both making excellent progress.

ANGELUS, July 1945

two very good friends, New Lands was purchased and the work there began to develop according to White Eagle's directions. The timing of his guidance on this, as on so many other matters, was exact, since even while negotiations were in progress for the purchase of the property, house prices began the upward spiral which has continued ever since.

New Lands was dedicated by White Eagle on 29 September (the Feast of St Michael and All Angels):

> Some forty of the brethren and members of the Lodge attended the service. The month of September granted its one perfect day's weather on that Saturday, and nothing marred any moment of it. Since then the spirit and the power are gathering within the chapel at New Lands. May it be that in the months and years to come the light will reach, help and bless many other lives. In his dedication White Eagle said, 'Beloved brethren, we in the spirit realm rejoice with you on this day of sunshine and power . . . This building is a home of peace and harmony and light. It has been prepared not for a few years but for centuries. Brethren of a very ancient Order have dwelt here before . . . We hope that in this house simplicity, harmony and brotherly love will ever be preserved. May all work together as a team . . . may the best always arise in the heart; and may God manifest through the brooms and the saucepans and the dusters of the home; may Christ manifest at the table, in the garden, in the flowers . . . Thus may there be established here a community of service, a Brotherhood of the ancient order of the Great White Light.
>
> ANGELUS, *November 1945*

Early views of New Lands chapel. The present side altar or Madonna altar was originally the main altar (above). Below a later picture, taken at the Christening of Colum and Jeremy Hayward in 1952.

Those who know New Lands today, who come in their cars past the Temple and sweep round the next bend into New Lands drive; who make, perhaps, for the office door, behind which they know are offices on three floors, housing a staff of twenty or more, will find it difficult to picture the New Lands of the late 1940s: unless, perhaps, they make for New Lands front door itself, or walk out into the garden; where, we hope, they can be sure that the monastic peace of New Lands is preserved. In those days there was only the one gateway from the road, the one into the gravelled drive at the top of the hill, through the oak gates hung on stone posts. This passed the back door (screened by trees and shrubs, as were the adjacent potting shed and greenhouses) before opening into the front drive. No road continued beyond as it does now: a high, thick conifer hedge which separated Garden Cottage from New Lands stretched right along the drive until it gave way to a little walk past the front lawn, beside an azalea bed.

The first retreat at New Lands was held in the week it opened, September 1945: but it was, at first, a summer centre; and a satellite, too, of the London Lodge. A thrilling and yet an exhausting task it was, getting the house together for the opening day; and an

NEW LANDS. When these lines are written the first visitors have yet to arrive at New Lands. What their impressions will be we do not of course know. Nor has the 29th of September come, which is to be the opening and dedication day of the house. Already preparations are far advanced, however, and wonderful is the way in which things have (more or less) arranged themselves in this the most difficult of all times to make preparation of a home.

ANGELUS, October 1945

added workload for Minesta, having a country house to run while her London commitments remained. There were twelve retreats in each of the first two or three summers, so we see her finishing a busy week in London and setting off for New Lands to prepare for a retreat which began on the Monday. She took a full part in the running of the house at first, even down to the ironing. As the farewells ceased at the end of the week, it was London again to think about, and a week which might include the monthly inner teaching or a White Eagle address on the Sunday. Ylana, as General Secretary of the Lodge, divided her time between London and New Lands (with Alison Innes often holding the fort in London in the meanwhile), and normally cooked for the Retreats. Joan was not so free to help, with a small child to look after; but John was 'demobbed' at the end of the War and, turning down a very good job in the world, threw himself wholeheartedly into the White Eagle work at a time when help was urgently needed. He was appointed Treasurer and was thus able to take over from Ylana part of the burden of her work. John remembers how White Eagle said to him when he came into the work, 'If you are going to work for White Eagle you have to be prepared to do anything'. He was, and he did!

John's task as Treasurer was no easy one. The cost of New Lands dwarfed the Lodge's resources, and the late 1940s and 1950s were a time of great stringency, in which the Lodge lived, even at the best of times, from hand to mouth; so John was constantly having to pay money from one Lodge account to another so that bills could be met. Often they were only met by a seeming miracle: an unexpected donation or a small legacy (this remains true today, although thankfully it now applies more to the extraordinary bills than the ordinary ones). The publications were in particular difficulty: little or no profit was made from sales, so there was no cash in hand for the publication of a new title, and one solution successfully tried in 1957 was the subscription scheme launched for the MORNING LIGHT series. But the greatest burden required more than the Treasurer's agility, and in a sense it also gave the greatest opportunity, for it brought the members together in a common effort.

This came in 1946. Hardly had we taken breath from the purchase of New Lands (and with its mortgage outstanding) than we were faced with the expiration of the lease on St Mary Abbots Place. However the owner, Mrs Calderon, who wished to sell, gave Minesta first refusal of an offer for the whole property (the two houses) for £15,000. We made a gesture of looking at other properties, but the guidance from the spirit was clear - that 9 St Mary Abbots Place was the Lodge home. So there was really no choice but to go forward in faith, as always; the offer was accepted, and a Building Fund launched; and in ANGELUS Minesta wrote:

I am happy to tell you that arrangements are in progress for the purchase of the present Lodge premises. The sum of £15,000 will be needed before we can have the building entirely free, as White Eagle has said it will be in due course, and of this sum we have to raise £6,000 before the end of May 1947. This will require every effort we can make [an understatement, we think].

ANGELUS, *November 1946*

In February 1947 we read: 'The day of completion of the purchase of the White Eagle Lodge building is May 7th next, so we have three months to go and £3,000 to raise. It is going to be a big task. We shall carry it through together.' And we did! The purchase was duly completed. But it was ten years and more of hard work, in which every one played their own part, before the mortgage, and the interest-free loans which had been so important to us in 1947, could be paid off. The financial struggle of 1947 had a far-reaching consequence beyond the London Lodge, for it hastened the Lodge's becoming a registered charity (which in turn made it possible to operate a Deed of Covenant scheme). It also produced the prototype of what has since become a tradition, namely our annual Christmas Fairs: a bring-and-buy sale held on 23 November 1946, followed by another at a hall in Hammersmith in April 1947.

1948 was important, for in that year came the first of a series of Trust Deeds by which not only both the Lodge properties but also the publications of the Lodge, the copyright of White Eagle's teachings, were transferred from private to public ownership to be held in Trust in perpetuity for the purposes laid down in the Deeds. This major step was not taken without much heart-searching by Minesta, as can be imagined, but it did mean that the Lodge could go forward guarded and guided by the ideals and principles first given to us by White Eagle. They placed the whole work on a secure foundation both materially and spiritually.

For this and very much more, we have to thank a true friend, referred to earlier, Noel Gabriel. His own spiritual insight coupled with a deep devotion to White Eagle and to White Eagle's medium, and later his knowledge of the law, were the gifts he brought to the work: and such gifts enabled him to formulate these various Trusts and to pilot them through the maze of legal formalities. He has served White Eagle devotedly since a young man, and it is hardly surprising therefore to read of White Eagle saying to him, during a group at the Lodge in 1938; 'Remember, my brother who studies the law, that you are preparing yourself as a channel for the White Brotherhood. You will be used in the service of the Brotherhood'.

Looking back down the years one of the remarkable things that stands out about the story of the Lodge is that always, when specialised knowledge and help has been needed, the right person has been there to give that help, and with it their heart. It is as

NEW LANDS. From July 29th to August 3rd there will be a particularly interesting course of instruction at New Lands, for Miss Betty Simpson and Miss Ann Cornock-Taylor, of the International Institute of Margaret Morris Movement, will be with us to instruct and to give demonstrations of their art and its relation to the health of man's vehicles, physical, mental and spiritual.

ANGELUS, July 1946

'THE SHINING PRESENCE.' After many months' delay the first cloth bound copies of this book have come to hand. A cloth bound book costs between three and four times as much to produce as in 1939.

ANGELUS, January 1947

though long before we all came into incarnation the plans were laid and each one detailed for his task.

But let us return to 1947, a very important year for the Lodge work in America. ANGELUS spoke of a Mrs Olive Robinson who

The first White Eagle Lodge of America, photographed in 1949

on a short visit to England last year, attended a service at the London Lodge and from that moment was inspired to carry White Eagle's teaching to the States and to found a Lodge in New Jersey. The result is a veritable proof of unwavering faith, courage and selfless service on her part and that of her husband who, guided . . . from the inner planes . . . brought into being the beautiful little temple now dedicated to the work . . .

The building . . . was constructed single-handed by Mr Robinson – even to the cutting of the timber and making the concrete blocks of which the walls are built, the installing of electric light and the plumbing. Working steadily from 4 a.m. each day throughout the intense heat of the summer the building gradually took shape and was completed by the opening date, August 17th 1947.

ANGELUS, *November 1947*

Alas – this, the first overseas Daughter Lodge, is no longer in being, for John Robinson passed over two or three years after its founding and although Olive continued with love and zeal for many years eventually the time came when age forced her to retire too. Nevertheless the seeds sown nearly forty years ago have borne rich fruit in the form of the many groups now all over the United States. It was at Olive's request that Brother Faithful produced the first Correspondence Course in Spiritual Unfoldment which she ran with happy effect for many years. A similar course is planned for the future, when the time is right.

In 1948 the first children's service was held in the Lodge, the beginning of the work with children which Joan began and which is now such a valuable and important aspect of the White Eagle work.

Another 'first' for 1948 was the formation of a group specially for the absent healing of animals; and some time later it is rather nice to read in ANGELUS of some of the cases.

On December 7th, 1949, the first meeting of the Astrological Lodge of the White Eagle Lodge was held. The aim of the group is the study of Astrology in all its branches but especially in connection with the spiritual unfoldment of man. There will be regular meetings at which instruction will be given, and also lectures of general astrological interest.

ANGELUS, January 1950

Pride of place had better be given to a Sealyham dog aged 14½ years, suffering, regrettably, from bad temper, having bitten various people – from which it may be argued that his teeth remain in good order. Since treatment by the group his temper has greatly improved.

Another patient was a parrot, suffering from sickness and moulting, which has recovered. Love and protection was also given to a young elephant over a period of several months when it was known that it was being cruelly treated while being trained. Results are not known in this case. Another loved dog was treated for shock after being knocked about by a gang of hooligans. He has now recovered, A huge Pyrenean dog suffering from eczema was also successfully treated.

ANGELUS, *October 1950*

In September 1949 came the first Chain of Fellowship article, a feature of ANGELUS and later of STELLA POLARIS which has continued ever since. In that first one Minesta wrote:

I hope to form a Chain with our ever-increasing family through-out the world as its link . . . Brief extracts will be given from the letters received, particularly from our readers overseas, so that there will follow a building-up of this family spirit through-out the world like that which we have endeavoured to establish at the London Lodge and the New Lands home. By this means, I hope all our readers will feel they are in personal touch and can share each others' interests.

ANGELUS, *September 1949*

Letters quoted came from Iceland, Australia, New Jersey and South Africa, so it will be seen how far White Eagle's teaching had already spread. The first of the much-loved 'Gentle Brother' series appeared in STELLA POLARIS in 1953.

A final memory of 1949 is the making of the first White Eagle gramophone record (now only to be found in our archives). It was a ten-inch record, running at 78 r.p.m., and it played for seven minutes. To the best of our memory it was made at the suggestion of a friend who had the recording equipment, which he brought to the Lodge with him. Recording was a very different and more taxing matter in those days than it is today with our magnetic tapes

PUBLICATIONS. We have to acknowledge with gratitude the gift of the sum of five hundred pounds towards our publications fund. This generous gift will enable us to proceed with the publication of 'The Living Word', White Eagle's interpretation of the Gospel of St. John.

ANGELUS, July 1948

New Lands, seen across one of the lawns in the early 1950s (or before). Note the huge wistaria on the side of the house, and the greenhouses, which have now given way for the office extension – little dreamt of then!

Ivan Cooke's painting of the line of beech trees that has so graced New Lands garden through our time there. There is another of Ivan Cooke's paintings visible on the picture on page 41.

which can be spliced and juggled with. The speaker had to record it just right, or forever hold his peace; and to the exact length. We remember White Eagle's patience and love as he repeated his message for the record two or three times in order to make the break at the appropriate moment. What amazed us was that although it was apparently spontaneous, each time he recorded it the words were to all intents and purposes the same. This certainty about his words was a very clear proof, if we needed one, that White Eagle was entirely separate from and superior to his medium.

When New Lands opened there was, of course, no local congregation, and no Lodge community there other than whichever members of Minesta's family happened to be there. Slowly, however, not only did the immediate family grow, but the wider family as well. Except in retreat weeks, the early Brotherhood ceremonies were never more than six strong, but these few brothers kept to their service faithfully through the 1950s. Among them were Frank and Beatrice Wharhirst, 'Frank' and 'Brown Lady', Minesta's brother-in-law and sister, who for the first few years lived actually on the estate at New Lands. A healing group was also held, chiefly with these same brothers. After the early years, the New Lands work grew faster, for under White Eagle's direction we began to hold activities in the winter months as well as during the summer. His instruction was that we should 'keep New Lands warm, on all planes' – and indeed a little community was growing, round New Lands, wanting regular services and groups. Thus a monthly Worship and Communion was started, and children's services and meditation groups.

Joan and John's second daughter Joan Minesta, now Jenny Dent, was born after the terrible winter of 1946-47 (a year marked for us also by the purchase of the London Lodge and by Brother Faithful's hospitalisation for a short period – something which had a good side to it, for it was in convalescence that he took up painting as a hobby and therapy).

In 1950 a new strength was brought into the work when Geoffrey Hayward joined the family. It was Geoffrey's support and clear understanding of White Eagle's vision of 'the home in the country' that had helped to give Minesta the courage to make that vision a reality. Coming from outside, he had an appreciation of the profundity and scope of White Eagle's teaching, and of the future of the work, which we who had our heads more buried in the business of every day probably lacked. On his marriage to Ylana he ceased his work as education officer in the R.A.F., and, like John before him, gave himself wholly to serving White Eagle and the Brotherhood. His coming was to have a profound effect on the work at many levels, but very particularly upon the books and publications, which were to become his special responsibility.

An event not entirely unconnected with his coming was the transformation of ANGELUS into the magazine you all know today, STELLA POLARIS, in December 1951. With the growing volume of work and increasing difficulties in the printing trade, it was becoming harder and harder to produce a monthly magazine. The cost of production was rising all the time, leading to an unacceptable subscription rate. We were being guided, too, to reach out to a greater public by including articles on a wider range of subjects (but with White Eagle's teaching always as the foundation). So STELLA POLARIS was born, with an entirely new format and clear typeface, to appear every two months; since when it has gone from strength to strength.

But we must go back to ANGELUS for a moment, for it was in February 1951 that the words of our Prayer for Humanity were made public and printed there. Probably this was the first time that all the White Eagle family had joined together in prayer to send out the Light, using the same words. Later came the 'call to prayer' at the magical hours, and the dedication to the service of the Light which has become so basic to the work.

In the same issue we read of Joan's election to the Board of the Faculty of Astrological Studies and of her earning the Faculty's Diploma – an indication of the important place of the study of the spiritual aspects and significance of the science of Astrology to the White Eagle work as a whole.

*

On 12th March we had a specially beautiful ceremony at the [London] Lodge, the first of its kind ever held. This was the ordination of two . . . Ministers who have served a long period of probation and training for their new office . . . Mrs Joan Hodgson (Joan Cooke) and Mrs Geoffrey Hayward (Ylana Cooke). Their ordination and dedication of their lives to the work of The White Eagle Lodge is particularly significant because they are also ordained as the future Trustees of the work of the White Eagle Lodge.

[And, in the same year:] John Hodgson, having served the required period of training and unfoldment, was ordained by White Eagle as a Minister of the White Eagle Lodge on July 2nd last. May a blessing rest upon his calling and his ministry.

ANGELUS, *April and September 1951*

With the steady increase of the activities at New Lands, the focus of the whole work began to change, and in 1953 all the administrative side of the work was moved down to the country. The volume of office work, both on the healing side (Joan) and for the General Secretary (Ylana) was such that it could no longer be done in a general reception office, which was all the space that London afforded. The move certainly made the work much easier – particu-

Your attention is drawn to the recital on Wednesday, January 24th, at 7 p.m. by Jean Sterling Mackinlay and Harcourt Williams who are generously giving their services for the Building fund. I know that all our friends will welcome the wonderful opportunity of hearing these two great artists in the spiritual atmosphere of the Lodge.

ANGELUS, January 1951

It is with great joy and thankfulness that we tell you of the birth of twin sons to Mr. and Mrs. Geoffrey Hayward (whom most of you will know as Geoffrey and Ylana). The little boys arrived on February 21st, and are extremely healthy and well . . . The little boys are to be called Joseph Colum and Arthur Jeremy.

From a list of activities and circular letter to members, June 1952

THE PERIOD OF THE CORONATION
As this period approaches we shall all be conscious of White Eagle's words concerning the deep significance of the Coronation not only for Britain but for all humanity.
STELLA POLARIS, April-May 1953

larly the despatch and storage of books, the volume of which was increasing all the time. We do wonder what we should have felt if we could have foreseen today's office extension!

In 1954 the first Garden Party at New Lands was held. It rained solidly and continually from early morning until the last guests departed. But somehow we managed to enjoy ourselves jamming every room and every passage of the house. Annette Mills (of Muffin the Mule fame) opened the Garden Party, nothing daunted. Her charm saved the day. We have since learnt to work on the weather and to seek the co-operation of the angels and the spirits of the sun, mostly with success!

Looking back, one thinks of the 1950s as difficult years – years of struggle to make ends meet, with the heavy burden of mortgage repayments overshadowing everything. As well as the running expenses, there was also the responsibility of the spiritual well-being of the whole work, both in London and at New Lands, which still fell largely upon Minesta, with Brother Faithful always beside her. The new ministers took their share, but were still very much in training, and their involvement was more with the secretarial and administrative than the spiritual side. That in itself was none too easy, with young families. Although she was quite seriously ill in 1956, we do not think Minesta's courage ever really failed her, and always White Eagle was strong and hopeful and forward-looking, bolstering our faith whenever it wavered; helping us all the time to understand spiritual law and to live with our vision on the Star. They were valuable, strengthening years, and prepared us for the further expansion of the 1960s.

May we remind readers particularly of the CHRISTMAS FAIR - to be opened by Lord Dowding at 2.30 p.m. on Saturday, November 20th, at the London Lodge, and that all gifts and donations should be sent there direct, as early as possible – and marked 'CHRISTMAS FAIR'.
STELLA POLARIS,
October-November 1954

*

In two years' time (that is, February 1957) the White Eagle Lodge will have carried on this work for twenty-one years . . . I think [this] calls for a special Anniversary celebration, and to mark this event it has been proposed to collect a Million Pennies as a Twenty-First Birthday Present to White Eagle's work . . . If *all* our 4000 friends would give 3d. a week for two years the Lodge will be freed of the heavy debt and funds will be freed to spread White Eagle's teaching . . .

In the entrance of the Lodge in London there stands the model of a Lighthouse, with a large collecting box. It will be lit from within, and as the number of pennies increases so the light will grow duly brighter.

We hope that this light will be the sign and symbol of the progress of the work of the White Eagle Lodge, both spiritually and materially.

Grace Cooke, in 'The Chain of Fellowship',
STELLA POLARIS, *April-May 1955*

Two years later the million pennies target was achieved; and a few months later, in time for our twenty-second anniversary, the London Lodge was finally cleared of all outstanding debt. Minesta promptly launched a second million penny fund, to help with the running expenses! She had a great belief in involving everyone in whatever project was on hand; in drawing us all together to meet a challenge so that everyone felt – and was – part of every venture. It was her inspiration that built up the wonderful family spirit that has grown and grown and remains the strength of the work.

A Garden Party of the mid-1950s. Note the camp fire, and Ylana leading visitors and a small choir in singing at the end.

In 1955 we produced the first of our annual Newsletters for Members. It took the form of a retrospective view of the previous year and appeared in duplicated form on three foolscap pages, close-typed. It was very much appreciated by Members everywhere, helping again to draw all together into a closer family; and also was specially appreciated by the growing number of overseas Members, for whom it brought the Lodge and its various activities close. An interesting point is made in this Newsletter:

> The character of the Sunday services has become more devotional by the substitution for the most part of a period of spiritual communion, for the usual clairvoyance. It is possible that this means that fewer of the general public are attracted to the Service, but we feel regular worshippers generally prefer the new form.
>
> *Retrospect 1954 (sent out 1955)*

Indeed they did, and congregations in fact grew.

1955 saw two major publications, the first to appear under the imprint of the newly-created White Eagle Publishing Trust (1953). They were HEALING (NOW HEALING BY THE SPIRIT), the printing of which was subsidised by two friends in the U.S.A.; and MEDITATION, which probably more than any other book to date set a standard and a guide to the White Eagle way of life, and sold more widely too. It broke new ground.

> It was during [the] war years that for a short time Minesta had the opportunity to study meditation according to Eastern methods. The teacher, obviously brought to her by White Eagle, helped her to see even more clearly the difference between what one might perhaps call spontaneous psychic gifts, and the conscious unfoldment of spiritual awareness through aspiration, and the mental discipline of meditation. For many years, White Eagle had been gradually bringing us to this point in his spiritual unfoldment groups, but contact with this teacher brought about an expansion of consciousness which enabled White Eagle to take us even further, henceforward the training was to become deeper and more along the lines described in Minesta's book MEDITATION.
>
> *Joan Hodgson, 'Personal Recollections of Minesta and White Eagle',*
> STELLA POLARIS, *August-September 1980*

Early retreat groups at New Lands: above, c.1951; below, 1956.

YOUNG PEOPLE'S GROUPS AT NEW
LANDS
We have held two Eaglet groups at
weekends this Spring . . . [The
Eaglets] are able to go together for
delightful country walks, they have
the companionship of each other
and interchange of thought; above
all, they have the opportunity of a
meditation group and a special
service on the Sunday afternoon.
STELLA POLARIS, June-July 1962

Retrospect 1956 makes the first mention of the group of young people (of whom there is never any shortage in the Lodge) drawn together as a working band, led by the enthusiasm and devotion of Michael Collishaw – still one of the strong pillars of the Lodge after more than thirty years in the Brotherhood – together with Diana Higgins and Edna Taylor, both now (to our loss) in the land of Light. They christened themselves – or was it White Eagle who christened them? – 'the Eaglets'; and many were their good works and their happy times together. Year after year they would come down to 'spring clean' New Lands and do various redecoration jobs; and in the London Lodge they mounted plays and entertainments for the enjoyment of members and the benefit of the funds. They would hold regular monthly discussions as well as enjoying many social occasions together; and at all the major Lodge functions the Eaglets were in evidence behind the scenes lending a hand. Although Michael now considers he is no longer a young person, the young people of the Lodge are still a very active force. They keep the London Lodge up to a high standard of decoration and take part in regular gardening weekends to help keep the Temple grounds in flowering order. And of course they are active in the spiritual work. We do not think we shall be short of workers in the future.

And so we come to 1957, the coming-of-age of the Lodge. In the previous year, in order to assist her convalescence, some good friends had taken Minesta and Faithful on holiday to France. While there they spent some time at Lordat, where they had worked with the Polaires twenty-five years previously. It was a very happy and powerful renewing of the old link and a touching again of the magic of the Polaire Star – almost, it seemed, a gift from the Brotherhood, of renewed strength and power for the coming-of-age.

Of the many announcements made in that year, perhaps the most significant was that about the creation of the Outer Brotherhood.

It is White Eagle's wish that an 'Outer Brotherhood' of the White Eagle Lodge be instituted in the New Year, under the symbol of the Star . . . If you have been a member for a year or longer [we now ask two years minimum] and are in sympathy with the ideal of an organised spiritual Brotherhood . . . will you write to me? You will then receive full particulars of this plan of the Wise Ones to form an outer membership of our Inner Brotherhood.
Grace Cooke, in STELLA POLARIS, *December 1956-January 1957*

More and more, as the years passed, people were coming into the Lodge because of the opportunity for service it offered. Uneasy world conditions, together with a growing spiritual awareness, stimulated this desire to serve. There was an increasing awakening

*Minesta at the Chateau of Lordat in
1931, on the Polaires' expedition there*

to the power of good thought and of the work with the Light which White Eagle had been teaching for so many years: also, the work of the Brotherhood had become known through some of the books. Thus, as people became attached to the Lodge and to the White Eagle path, many felt the call to dedicate themselves wholly to this inner service under the magic of the Star. Before 1957, only those living close enough to a Lodge to be able to attend regularly were eligible for it. White Eagle's guidance that an 'outer' circle of the Brotherhood should be called together meant that this work was open to all who proved themselves to be truly dedicated: an opportunity to any member, even if he or she lived on the other side of the world, to become part of the great chain of Brotherhood which does indeed now stretch round the world. The first initiations into this special work took place on 11 March, and ever since the band of Outer Brothers has grown steadily.

On the publishing side, a contribution to the twenty-first birthday was the issue of a bibliography of all the White Eagle publications, starting with THE HEAVENS ARE RINGING, Brother Faithful's story of the Burstow ghost, published in 1930. But the most significant event of 1957 was the launch of what was called 'the Cheap Book Series', beginning with MORNING LIGHT. The conception was Geoffrey Hayward's. Conscious of the high cost of producing a book – the most recent, THE RETURN OF ARTHUR CONAN DOYLE, a revised edition of THY KINGDOM COME, to commemorate the twenty-first birthday, had had to sell at 15s 0d, rather more than our own members or most Spiritualists could easily afford – he looked for ways of producing a pocket hardback book which could sell for as little as the 5s 0d MORNING LIGHT cost when it appeared. The conception also was to produce a book complete in itself in which extracts from White Eagle's teaching were grouped around a particular theme or for a particular purpose. This was an instruction White Eagle himself had given us: a book which would help those starting on the spiritual path (this was MORNING LIGHT); another, which looked towards what lies at the end of that path (GOLDEN HARVEST, published in 1958); and a third, describing the higher worlds, for those afraid of death particularly, or affected by bereavement (SUNRISE, 1958). Later HEAL THYSELF was added to the series (1962) and finally the bedside book of White Eagle readings, THE GENTLE BROTHER (1968).

Looking back on these publications, we realise what a revolution they represent. Breaking away from the old style of book – the large collections of teaching – they gave an enhanced feeling of light and clarity and have formed the pattern for nearly all our books since then. They also proved valuable sources of readings in churches and for groups inside and outside the White Eagle Lodge. This, along with the price, led to increased sales as hoped,

CONTENTS

Contents page of MORNING LIGHT

which in turn gave opportunities for further expansion. They thus formed the foundation of the huge increase in sales of all the books in the 1960s and 1970s.

The feeling of 'light and clarity' arose from another aspect of the books beside the editing, that of design. Although we look at the very early White Eagle books with great pleasure – we were very fortunate with our early illustrators and printers, and some of the books have a pleasing 'Arts and Crafts' feel to them – this kind of production was quite uneconomical in the fifties, if indeed it was even possible. With the War, standards had fallen badly and although considerable effort was spent on MEDITATION and HEALING in 1955, it was the Cheap Book Series that really provided the new standard. Geoffrey's design used a large and attractively individual typeface on a smallish page with good margins. All was neatly done, and the book was bound in a cream-coloured imitation vellum wrapped in cellophane to give it a sparkle (this tended to get damaged and was eventually replaced by a paper jacket).

In the new wave of publications another brother may be mentioned. Keith Ellis worked with a large East Anglian book printer, and was so stirred by the poor appearance of one of the early post-war books, he offered his services when appropriate. It was another instance of someone being sent at just the right time. Not only did his advice open up new possibilities, it also enabled us to save money while actually increasing quality, and continues to do so.

*

We have recently completed the preparation of a geographical posting list. This means that we now have the names and addresses of all our members and friends not only listed alphabetically but also grouped together in a separate index under the countries and counties and towns in which they live. Of course we never divulge a name or address without the owner's permission, but this new index means that we can now more easily link you with other friends in your neighbourhood should you

Left, Minesta and Brother Faithful cut the 'lighthouse' cake at our twenty-first birthday celebrations; right, The White Eagle Choir singing at the Twenty-First Anniversary Service in March 1957. Note the organ in its then position to the right of the altar

be interested in forming a group for the study of White Eagle's teaching.

STELLA POLARIS, *February-March 1957*

This was a more mundane event than the other events of 1957 but one which probably contributed more than any other single factor to the growth of the group work all over the world in the decade following.

Not a great deal has been said to date about the healing work, growing quietly but steadily through the years. By 1959 the original two absent healing groups had grown to forty or more, a number which included thirteen groups sitting on their own in other parts of the country. Through all the early years the contact healing was given entirely by individual healers in private chapels. Joan well remembers, because this side of the work has always been her special care, White Eagle's masterly handling of each patient who came for diagnosis (before receiving treatment). 'He seemed to look right into their hearts and by his love to melt away the fears and conflicts which beset them and were of course the basic cause of the physical inharmony.' In 1954 these private sessions were replaced by a monthly healing service conducted by White Eagle, when first he spoke generally and then gave individual diagnoses to about six patients, allotting them healers there and then, with full instructions for their treatment. This monthly healing meeting developed into a service for the laying-on-of-hands, taken by White Eagle. At these services he gave a talk to patients and healers, and at a certain point the patients were called forward and the healers treated them by just holding their hands above the patient's head.

In 1959 and under White Eagle's guidance the contact healing work was reorganised into its present form. The monthly service and the private treatments were replaced by a daily healing service at which the patients were treated by White Eagle's colour method according to their individual needs.

With this change came another, for the monthly healing service became the service of communion and dedication, purely for Lodge healers, which remains an essential part of the White Eagle healing work and means so much to us all. People find them 'oases of blessing and refreshment, from which the participants emerge recharged and inspired to keep on keeping on faithfully with their loving service to humanity' (Retrospect 1960).

Retrospect 1960 also announced the launching of the Lone Healing scheme.

For some years now a few members who were prevented by circumstances from sitting in an absent healing group at one of the Lodges have been linking in to certain groups as absentee sitters. As the numbers of those longing to serve in this way are

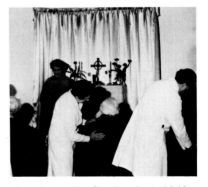

At a Contact Healing Service (c.1968)

MORNING LIGHT IN DUTCH
We are glad to announce that this book will be available in Dutch by November 1st. The translation is by Miss Charlotte van Nievelt of The Hague, and the Dutch title of the book is MORGEN-LICHT.

STELLA POLARIS,
October-November 1958

*An Absent Healing group in the then
White Eagle Chapel (c.1968)*

growing, we are guided to form a special group for 'Lone Healers', which will give to those of you who feel cut off from the Lodge activities a chance to serve in a unique way, at the day and time of your own choice. If you would like to become a 'White Eagle Lone Healer' please write to the Secretary for further particulars.

This was a milestone indeed in the White Eagle service, for the lone healing work now stretches across the world.

It was in this Newsletter (the healing planets must have been shining brightly) that we printed an appeal White Eagle had made,

'There will be a period of silent communion and prayer (at New Lands) every day until there is a spiritual atmosphere, a holy centre of power to which all may come and really touch and see and know God. This is the purpose of the work, the building up of the invisible life-force which will be like a great fountain blessing all souls who are guided here by the invisible Brotherhood whom you serve.'

So now, not only on Christmas morning but every morning at twelve o'clock, this call to communion in the chapel at New Lands goes out and those who are on the estate at the time answer the call. We believe you will like to think of this ever-burning light at New Lands and that you will sometimes join us in spirit at these times to give and to receive the blessing.

Thus it was that the twelve noon call to prayer and to send out the Light which had been such a feature of the early wartime era was reborn in our Silver Jubilee year, and is today observed by followers of our teaching all over the world. The little light on the altar at New Lands never goes out, it is a constant flame.

At the purely material level the mortgage debt on New Lands was finally cleared before the Silver Jubilee celebrations. And also by the generosity of members three improvements were made at St Mary Abbots Place, reported by Minesta in her 'Chain of Fellowship' for December 1961. One, the installation of adequate oil heating, at last, so that 'the Lodge will henceforth be cosily and cleanly warmed throughout'. Two, new wood-block flooring: 'For how many years have we all endured with exemplary stoicism, cold feet and shivering backs, due to the damp rising through the cold stone floor! Now all will be warm and dry'. Three, a new central chandelier for the main chapel. It need hardly be said that all three gifts were, quite literally, warmly appreciated.

4

The Temple

How CAN we measure the progress of a spiritual work such as this? Not by the numbers and publicity it attracts. Progress is measured by the effect on every individual life that the light of the Lodge reaches – here or on the other side of the world. All who come into the White Eagle Lodge to worship and to serve must grow in the inward grace, or in inward power to affect the lives of others . . .

The purpose of our work here is that every soul who enters the Lodge, every soul who participates in the work, shall grow in spiritual power, which will radiate from him to give light and healing to the world. Remember – it is not what comes from the lips, but from the heart, which can inspire a life with love and joy and peace. The White Eagle work should be as leaven in the bread of life to the world.

White Eagle

*

STELLA POLARIS for April 1961 has a simple silver cover with the title picked out in blue and our rose-star symbol above it. Beneath are the words 'The White Eagle Lodge Silver Jubilee'. Twenty-five rather eventful years of Lodge history had gone by, and the Lodge had come out of them with an identity very close to what it has today, despite the enormous growth that has occurred since; rather as a person's character is moulded in adolescence but shows more clearly in the twenties, when the soul becomes fully incarnated.

We marked the Jubilee with a special service – some of White Eagle's words then were given at the beginning of this book – and also with a merry party at the London Lodge, held on the very anniversary itself, 22 February 1961. 'The first thing that we all saw as we entered the Lodge', says the account in STELLA POLARIS, 'was the great silver star against the dark blue background of the curtains, with silver rays reaching down to meet the glorious display of flowers and greetings arranged below'. Our Brother 'Mark', Paul Beard, proposed a toast, comparing the Lodge to 'a broad, great big sheltering oak tree'. Brother Faithful picked this up in his reply, and reminded us of the strength of an oak. But the strength, he said, lay in the devoted service given by members and friends of the Lodge. 'I do not undervalue the financial, the material help – that indeed has been generous and kind; but the most precious gift anyone can give is their life for the White Eagle work; their constant service, their love, their sympathy, their friendship'. But it is to Minesta's own speech that we turn particularly:

New Lands from the air (1956 or earlier)

When this Lodge was called into being, White Eagle said: 'You build on the four-square'. Well, there happened to be just four of us in the family at that time. But he meant far more than four-square people. The four-square base is perfect . . . And we must remember to apply this . . . to our dealings with our fellow men: be always on the square, be true and straight . . . From the four-square base – right living, right thought, right speech, right action – comes the pyramid of spiritual Light, the development of the spirit. And then the spirit sees the vision of the perfect six-pointed star-symbol of the Christ-man, or the perfected soul. I would like to hold this symbol before you all. May everyone of us pray to have the strength and the vision to act and live and serve on the square.

A message equally apposite at our Golden Jubilee.

The family had been four, and with John Hodgson and Geoffrey Hayward it had increased to six, but the following year the number of the family involved in the running of the Lodge rose to seven with the first of the next generation, Rose, entering the work as Minesta's personal secretary – as well as taking on the cooking for the retreat weeks at New Lands, a job which cannot have seemed more than a humdrum task at the time, but which was to have remarkable consequences! Rose, only 17 at the time, had her sights on university and cannot have foreseen what the change of plan would lead to. She became engaged that same year, to Anthony Elliot, the son of 'Mary' and 'John', leaders of the Plymouth Lodge, and they were married in the London Lodge on 24 August 1963.

This period is also marked by important developments in the healing work and in the running of the Lodge. For a long time, the only secretarial help we had had was that of the irreplaceable Alison Innes, Sister 'Pearl', as a personal assistant (and also as the most meticulous of proof-readers), and of Margaret Ross, a remarkably capable secretary, who ran the General Office (with our staff of today it is incredible to think of the clerical work, including the typing and duplicating of White Eagle's weekly teachings, being done by one person). Late in 1960, however, we took on in addition Isobel Hutchings, whose assistance made possible a major reorganisation of the absent healing administration. From this period, for instance, dates the system of maintaining proper reports on patients' progress, and an efficient system of adhesive slips by which patients could be added to the healing lists.

Very influential in these changes were some of our brothers who were drawing close to help the work. Rosemary and Paul Beard suggested several of the improvements, and Peter and 'Billie' Hamilton (Moonflower, as everyone knows her) dealt with some of the correspondence with patients. Other brothers helped in typing lists, and with the Lone Healing. But the greatest contribution of the brothers we have mentioned was in the day-to-day running of the London Lodge, where Peter and Moonflower and Paul and Rosemary, each as a pair, took charge for individual days of the week and enabled Minesta's family to devote more time to the country centre. Paul also looked after the fabric of the building with a professional's eye.

One of whom special mention must be made is Sister 'Radiance' (Irene Hancock) for she is one of the very few still with us today whose links, so far as this incarnation are concerned, go back to the days before even the Lodge started. Her wartime work limited the amount she was able to do in those early years, but after the War she gave more and more time to White Eagle.

In 1948 she came to live in one of the flats in 9a St Mary Abbots Place and during succeeding years her work in the London Lodge built up to the point where she was taking overall care, as the family became increasingly involved at New Lands. The extent of her contribution to the work, in loving and selfless service in many different ways and at all levels, it would be impossible to overstate. So many have come to know and love her over the years and have turned to her as a friend in need, and they will join us, we know, in paying loving and thankful tribute to her.

Another great server was Sister 'Peace' (Enid Brown) who took early retirement from her career to devote herself wholly to the Lodge work. In the early 1960s she completely reorganised and reclassified the London Lodge library and set it on the footing it has today. Today her spirit presence is still with us and many have felt an unseen hand guiding them as they use the library. A Sister, 'Serena' (Marian Bumford), recorded White Eagle's Sunday Addresses meticulously for more than 20 years and our debt to her is considerable.

There were many, many others, of course, for the work was growing all the time – willing helpers whose work and devotion are built into the very fabric of the Lodge. It is not possible to name them all, but in our hearts they will always be remembered.

A time of growth and a time of loss, which paradox was never so particularly felt as in 1965. On 2 March Rose gave birth to Katharine, her first daughter and Minesta's first great grand-child. But in January 'Mark' (Paul Beard) left us to give a decade of his life to the administration of the College of Psychic Studies in South Kensington. Two months later Geoffrey Hayward's destiny took him away from the family group and from the running of the Lodge, after he had endowed it with the deep gifts of his vision – and of his own practical ability, in the production of books. But at this time also there had come into the work Jenny, fresh from school and college, and she started by taking on much of the responsibility which Rose, with a young child, was now unable to carry. To Jenny we owe the help, over a crucial period, of Stuart

[Twenty-Seventh Anniversary Members' Party:] During the proceedings, our valued Brother 'Nobleheart' [Sir Ronald Fraser], in proposing a toast to the future of the work, spoke of his journey last year to South Africa. He said how deeply he missed his frequent attendance at the healing work at the London Lodge. On his journey back, however, he called in at the Nairobi W.E. group and he described to us the wonderful welcome he experienced as soon as he entered the sanctuary there: 'There it was, exactly as we feel it in the London Lodge – the spiritual power and peace was quite unmistakable'.

STELLA POLARIS, April-May 1963

Neil, who took on some of Geoffrey Hayward's responsibility for the running of the 'business' of the Publishing Trust (and in the process reformed its accounting and stock control systems). To Jenny we also owe the bringing of Geoffrey Dent full-time into the work in 1972. It was he who permanently took on the business management of the Publishing Trust, and who helped to lighten John (Hodgson) of his huge load with the Lodge accounts, eventually becoming Treasurer of the Lodge in 1979. Geoffrey and Jenny were married in the London Lodge on 11 April 1970.

Perhaps this awareness that a new generation was emerging is also symbolised in Joan's book WHY ON EARTH, which was published in 1964. Written at the request of, and partly financed by, the 'Eaglets', it was originally to be entitled 'Light on the Hills' (the much punchier title was suggested by John) and carried the subtitle 'The Light of the Ancient Wisdom on Modern Problems'. It thus formed an introductory book about White Eagle's teaching, and at the same time drew on the teaching to give a moral lead in the permissive 1960s. It was much revised in 1978 and remains popular today.

The dedication of the Lodge at The Hague. Mrs Petri-Moora is seated, right

A visit to the Worthing Lodge by Minesta and Faithful, with Ylana and Joan. The Worthing Lodge leader, Sister 'Felicia', Eve Wilson, stands on Brother Faithful's right.

HOLLAND, THE HAGUE. Saturday, October 16th, 1965, was indeed a memorable occasion for the Dutch Group at The Hague. On this day White Eagle spoke to over fifty people at the dedication ceremony. More had wished to attend but could not be accommodated in this beautiful sanctuary. All day long flowers had arrived from friends in Holland and in England, bringing their own message of love; and blessing, both for this centre and for White Eagle.

STELLA POLARIS, *December 1965–January 1966*

The Dutch Lodge was the second overseas Daughter Lodge and was largely the result of the tireless efforts of its leader, Margaret Petri-Moora. White Eagle spoke memorably on this occasion, which was the first time Minesta had travelled overseas on Lodge business, and marked in a general way the beginning of an era. There was a significant growth in the number of Daughter Lodges in the early 1960s with Worthing, Ascot and Reading also joining those of the 1940s (Edinburgh, Glasgow and New Jersey) and 1950s (Bournemouth and Plymouth).

These developments in the worldwide work are an indication of a general expansion in the 1960s which has continued. Undoubtedly one of the catalysts later in the decade was the launch of the Affiliation Scheme in 1966. This was designed to enable independent groups of servers to associate themselves with the White Eagle family, but its chief effect was to encourage individuals to start White Eagle groups, either to do their healing work with others, or to provide opportunities for discussion and meditation. Affiliation remains the first step towards the eventual establishment of a fully-fledged White Eagle Group or Daughter Lodge.

1966 was a momentous year, partly because of the Affiliation Scheme, and partly because of the extensive restructuring of the London Lodge that was completed late that year. Although the main chapel, Brotherhood Chapel and present library have been little altered over the years (though the library has been both sitting room and chapel), most of the other rooms, in shape and in use, date from the building works of 1966. But the main reason for the significance of 1966 lies elsewhere.

At the Thirtieth Anniversary Service White Eagle spoke as usual, but Sir Arthur Conan Doyle came very close too, and seemed to give the service special power. White Eagle kept his surprise for us till the end of his message:

The London Lodge library, shortly after the redecoration and rebuilding of 1966

> Now, turn your mind to our centre in the country, to New Lands, which stands on the hill. Upon that hill we are holding in thought, we see being built in the ether, a simple but pure temple through which will flow increasing heavenly wisdom and power – which will become a centre of life, a centre of light.
>
> We therefore charge all our brethren, all members and friends, to come in and help us to erect our temple on the hill-top, just as the temples were built in ancient days, which served their purpose, though they have now crumbled away. This temple has a still greater purpose to serve, long after those of you here will be with us in the spirit. This must be your gift, and our gift to coming generations.
>
> *Reprinted in* STELLA POLARIS, *June–July 1966*

What a charge! Yet it was not one for which White Eagle's family were totally unprepared. The story, told by Ivan Cooke in THE TEMPLE ANGEL, seemed to go back to their first years at New Lands. Minesta had had a dream then, in which she was led to a monastery in Italy, overlooking the Mediterranean. A monk in a white habit, whom she knew to be a saint of the early Christian Brotherhood, greeted her, and pointed up the hill before them, as if indicating 'that there were greater heights to climb and more work still to be done for the Brotherhood'. The dream remained with her. In 1965, at the instigation of a brother of the Lodge, Minesta and Faithful set off to Italy to find the monastery. Finding it by a happy piece of guidance, she was again visited by the saintly monk.

> We were told that the work had come to a point of change, and fresh power and inspiration were needed. We had been brought here for this purpose to give us further insight into the plan. A new phase was coming into the work of the White Eagle Lodge, greater power, more revelation, further proofs. We were given further insight into the Star Brotherhood, its power and its light. We were shown a vision of the inner meaning of the brotherhood

The next Open Evening will be on March 8th when our good friend Philip Jones will explain and demonstrate the working of the new organ. [Philip Jones later became Lodge organist and since the opening of the Temple has given his services there, to our great enrichment.]

We specially draw attention to the Inner Teaching by White Eagle on *Tuesday, February 8th*. Inner Teachings have now become rather a rare event in the London Lodge calendar, so this is something not to be missed.

STELLA POLARIS,
February-March 1966

WORSHIP THROUGH SINGING
Sunday, July 17th, saw an
innovation at the London Lodge
for on this occasion the first service
of 'Worship through Singing' was
held. The service took the form of
specially chosen hymns
interspersed with prayers and short
readings from White Eagle's
teaching again specially selected to
help the congregation appreciate
the hymns and worship fully
through their beautiful words and
music.

STELLA POLARIS,
August-September 1966

of all life, not only of brotherhood between men on earth, but
the brotherhood of men and angels, the brotherhood of men
with nature, with the solar life. We were told that through the
past twenty-five years we had been upheld and maintained by
the power of the Star, waiting for the time when further progress
was to be made toward the establishment of the Star Brotherhood
on earth.

Referring to the work at New Lands, it was said that New
Lands would become an unusual and powerful spiritual centre,
and that a new chapel, or temple, was to be built on the hill. It
would be world-known in the years to come.

Ivan Cooke, THE TEMPLE ANGEL

This was the first clear intimation given to Minesta about the
Temple, but it is apparent to us now that the Brothers in spirit had
held the plan for many earthly years. We recall, for instance, some
of White Eagle's words to Minesta's family on New Year's Eve in
1944, the occasion on which he told them about New Lands. The
full significance of his words, however, can hardly have reached
them.

It will be in the year 1945 that a light will be lighted in the history
of the White Brotherhood, of the White Eagle Lodge. You will
lay the foundation in this year upon which will be erected a pure
White Temple which will live, which will remain standing and
which will expand and grow in influence long after you have left
your present body . . . It is a work with a small beginning, but a
vast future. We foresee, we hope, that the chapel will be a place
of meditation, a meeting place between heaven and earth.

Reprinted in Newsletter, February 1966

But there is an even more remarkable story to tell, for it goes
back well before the Lodge itself came into being. We have written
already of Mabel Beatty's circle, which Minesta was invited to join
in 1930. Records of Mrs Beatty's circle from April that year to
January 1931, during which period White Eagle spoke on most
occasions, remained forgotten until we began work on this book.
But we find that on 4 April 1930 Minesta, in semi-trance, gave a
message which must, at the time, have been rather an enigma. Her
words were:

We tell you again that one is coming to you from across the
water – one who has great knowledge and wisdom – he is
coming to you. [This must be a reference to the Polaire messenger.]
I can see a white building which will stand in London. No – not
London – but [the] foundation is in London. The white building
is peaceful and quiet.

Truly a remarkable prophecy.

*

And so a new period of fund-raising began.

While we were busy collecting our first 'million sixpences' for the Temple building fund, Rose was engaged on another task as well. Over the twenty years New Lands had been run as a retreat centre, we had accumulated quite a collection of vegetarian recipes, all tried and tested and with the New Lands stamp. White Eagle has always advocated progressive change to a vegetarian diet (it was Rose herself, in childhood, who finally brought the family off fish) and had given us a vision of a time to come, not so far in the future, when no one will eat meat. Indeed, in 1970 he stated prophetically that in the next decade people would turn to vegetarianism because there wouldn't be enough meat to feed them – something borne out by the growing realisation now that only crops use land sufficiently economically to be feeding the world. (Also at this time, two New Lands brothers felt moved to start an organization promoting greater awareness in agriculture of the needs of animals and of the soil. Compassion in World Farming was formed in 1967 and Minesta and Faithful were two of its founder-Trustees.)

Rose took up the challenge, for we all felt that the Lodge had a part to play in facilitating the great change of attitude that was to come. Experimenting, adding her own genius and easy literary style to the recipe ideas worked out for the retreats, she produced a cookbook, SIMPLY DELICIOUS, in 1967. It was an entirely new venture for the Publishing Trust, and no one was quite prepared for the success it had. Five years later Rose wrote NOT JUST A LOAD OF OLD LENTILS (the title arose from a chance remark to the book's illustrator, in a shop), which was the book eventually spotted by Fontana. Today Rose's books have sold over three-quarters of a million copies, the bulk of them through Fontana, and she must have done as much as any writer in Britain to promote the image of vegetarianism.

Rose's books had an important effect on our development, for they introduced New Lands and the Lodge to a much wider circle. Many members today owe their introduction to SIMPLY DELICIOUS, which in its first full year of publication sold as many copies as all our titles put together had sold only three years previously. We were also producing books regularly, at least one new one every year and sometimes two. Our overall sales rose from a steady 3000 in the early 1960s to over 10,000 by 1970. Yet those increases pale beside those of the 1970s, which have a different cause.

Ever since the first bulk order of ILLUMINATION was despatched to New York in the 1930s, sales of the books in the U.S.A. had been growing, and by the early 1970s we had two distributors taking several thousand copies between them. Then we lost them both – and gained another, De Vorss of California. Though our relationship began slowly, it soon 'took off' and today the number of books

[Launch of the Million Sixpence Fund.] Of course this cannot be done without effort, without selflessness, without money. We have to be very practical. From this rostrum we now ask you all to bring your silver sixpences as a gift. Every time a silver sixpence comes your way bring it here to put in a little box. Now, dear friends, we must set ourselves to collect *one million silver sixpences*! and if you will set your mind to it we shall get our million sixpences as if by magic. Just you see, just you try; and as you put each sixpence of yours in the box, probably *we* shall put two sixpences in just as a little encouragement. Please, this is our Anniversary request.

White Eagle's address at the Thirtieth Anniversary Service, 6 March 1966, printed in STELLA POLARIS, June-July 1966 sold in the U.S.A., through De Vorss and elsewhere, is huge.

Just prior to this – in 1972 – we produced a book of White Eagle's teaching which, quite unexpectedly, was a breakthrough in getting White Eagle's message through to the general public. As an indication of its success in this, some of the passages in the book are reprinted in a U.S. Navy chaplaincy prayer book, a collection for use in prisons, and in a devotional collection produced by one of the English universities. The book is also used in the care of the dying. We leave Ylana to tell the story of THE QUIET MIND.

'Every White Eagle book has its own memories, but THE QUIET MIND particularly stands out because of the way its compilation was, in effect, taken out of my hands. The popularity of White Eagle's Calendar and the great help it was proving to its readers suggested that a book of his collected sayings would be valuable. It sounds easy enough, but you can't just throw "sayings" together haphazardly – and how to arrange them in any sort of order? I tried this way and that for days but nothing seemed right, and I began to despair and feel the book wasn't "on". I went to sleep one night with a prayer in my heart for guidance. Next morning I woke early with an inner voice saying "The secret of strength lies in the quiet mind . . ." I knew immediately that "The Quiet Mind" was the title and that White Eagle was leading me to the passage in MEDITATION which begins with those words.

'I read the passage, found it fell beautifully into headings; went to my work table where all the White Eagle sayings were laid out, and in no time at all they were sorted under those headings – and from the hundreds of sayings the right ones seemed to present themselves and fall into order. By lunchtime, the task was complete, apart from writing the introduction, and my heart was singing!'

By 1980, sales of the religious books had risen to over 55,000 p.a., with the vegetarian books accounting for another 13,000 (by this time we were already running down our distribution of cookery books, as Fontana could obviously do it more effectively than we could). Today, as many as sixty per cent are sent overseas. Many of these are to the U.S.A., but the sales in Australasia are also large and we have distributors in South Africa and Nigeria. In the despatch of these books we must record (among others) the service of Charles Waters, our Brother 'James', who retired at the age of 80 in 1973, having seen his job grow from the packing of four or five thousand books a year to about 40,000! In other countries the translations boost the dissemination of the White Eagle teachings very considerably, particularly in Germany and Switzerland where the tireless work of two Brothers, Walter and Edith Ohr, has brought about a very wide distribution of the books. Their effort is mirrored in other countries where friends have laboured to bring out translations of the books: Sweden, France and Holland especially.

The first work on the Temple was the construction of an approach road

TWO NEW BOOKS: Next month (November) two exciting new books are appearing. The first, a book for children, by Joan Hodgson, all in colour . . . HULLO SUN. And then the magnificent successor to SIMPLY DELICIOUS which sets out to prove – and triumphantly succeeds in its task! – that vegetarian cookery is NOT JUST A LOAD OF OLD LENTILS!
STELLA POLARIS,
October-November 1972

In all, White Eagle books are now translated into no less than eleven languages besides English and we thank all who have made this work part of their service.

During the same period there has been a comparable expansion in the membership of the Lodge. Our first annual newsletter, in 1955, referred to 376 members, of whom only 163 lived so far away they could not attend the London Lodge. In February 1966, our newsletter recorded 694. By 1973, the figure had doubled to 1536; and it doubled again to reach the 3000 mark in 1980. Today we have topped 5000. The regional groups have grown in number similarly. There were 29 groups and Lodges in 1964. The affiliation scheme brought 14 new groups in its first two years; and by 1974 there were 80 groups in all – but 107 in 1978 and 132 in 1982. There are now 175 of them. Daughter Lodges were established in Teignmouth in 1971, in Crowborough in 1975, and in Ipswich in 1976. Our Brisbane, Australia, Lodge dates from 1976 and there was one in Epping, N.S.W., from 1968 to 1973.

This huge expansion meant an equally sudden expansion in the workload, and our memories of the late 1960s and 1970s are dominated by coping with the numbers – at all levels.

First, the numbers we had to fit in New Lands Chapel for Sunday services before the Temple was built. Any festival service involved chairs and a public address system in New Lands lounge, and on occasion in the hall and dining room as well.

Then there were the huge number of advertising leaflets for the books which had to be printed. In those days, many more magazines than now took loose leaf insertions, and as a Brother had made a gift of the cost of a small offset printing machine in 1965 (in its effects, one of the more revolutionary gifts we have received), we were – workload apart – ideally placed to print literally hundreds of thousands of leaflets. Colum and Jeremy remember many school holidays with their hands blue with printing ink!

Lastly, there were those million sixpences – and more! to be raised to build the Temple. When White Eagle gave us his vision it seemed daunting financially. But if we raised a million sixpences, as we had twice raised a million pennies (Britain was still using pounds, shillings and pence until 1971), we would be well on the way to paying for the Temple; and as he had said, maybe for every sixpence that we on earth put in they in spirit would put in two. This really is how it was all through those seemingly endless days of fund-raising; every time we counted the total of an individual campaign or fund-raising event, it always seemed a bit bigger than we'd expected. Almost the whole sum of the Temple Fund was made up of small amounts. Not all of them were sixpences, but 'T.M.S.F. (K.O.K.O)', the mystic initials we gave the fund, symbolise it all: 'The Million Sixpence Fund (Keep On Keeping On)'!

'SING A SONG OF SIXPENCE'
This was the title of the delightful and highly entertaining Revue written and presented by the White Eagle Lodge Drama Group in aid of the Million Sixpence Fund on Friday and Saturday, October 20th and 21st. Native inspiration and months of hard work combined to produce a really first class show whose wit was equalled by its charm
STELLA POLARIS,
December 1967-January 1968

May we draw your attention to White Eagle's record, which is now available? It runs for 30 minutes' playing time and is, we think, a near perfect reproduction of White Eagle's actual voice, speaking through Mrs Cooke. White Eagle seems to come very close as one listens to his record.

STELLA POLARIS, June-July 1968

THE LONDON LODGE: IMPORTANT. A recent survey of the London Lodge premises has revealed extensive and active dry rot in part of the fabric . . . Not only will the work involve us in the expenditure of many hundreds of pounds, but it will also mean that the date of the re-opening of the Lodge after the Christmas break cannot certainly be fixed.

STELLA POLARIS, December 1969-January 1970

The discovery of dry rot in London at the very outset of the Temple appeal was a very serious blow and eventually cost not many hundreds but many thousands. One of our chief memories, apart from the dirt and the smell, was of Minesta's courage and steadiness, riding the storm.

Members, groups and Lodges organised numerous fund-raising events – coffee mornings, evening parties, raffles and concerts; the children at New Lands held a sponsored silence; and individuals painted pictures, or sold crafts; we collected stamps, coins, anything! But no idea has had quite such a lasting effect as the sponsored walk, which was instituted in 1970 and has been an annual event at Michaelmas ever since. Always intended as a day on the Downs in the fresh air first, and a fund-raising activity second, it nonetheless snowballed (to borrow a term from the one type of weather we haven't had on the walk!) and it has been one of the most successful ways of raising funds. Much tribute is due to all who braved blisters and bruises for the Appeal; and to those whose sponsorship was always a sacrifice, however small or great.

We are very proud of the generosity of our members, and to have raised (in all the many ways we have described) over £140,000 in ten years until the cost of the Temple was paid off, is a wonderful achievement.

In all the fund-raising, the younger generation took the lead in organising events and producing ideas. But there is one of them whose contribution to the building of the Temple was a very special one: Anthony Elliot (today he prefers to be called Robert) who came into the work in 1969. Anthony had first given us the benefit of his technical knowledge when the major reorganisation of the London building was carried out in 1966. He also inspired us to promote the Lodge teaching more widely, drew us our Lodge symbol, and drafted the 'blue star leaflet' about the Lodge. He saw into print the eight booklets about our teaching which are still standard ('A Brief Outline of White Eagle's Teaching', etc.) and he made an outstanding contribution to the work with his skilful recordings of White Eagle's talks, some of which he later produced as our first L.P. records – and our first tape cassettes. But the seven years he took off from his job at Plessey were principally to see through the building of the White Temple.

It was not an easy task, neither for Anthony nor any member of the family. The original architects' very imaginative plan had eventually to be dropped – it was just too radical. In rather difficult circumstances we turned to a Lodge member whose expertise as an architect had been proven in the design of two of London's theatres, Elidir Davies. White Eagle told us that the Brothers in spirit could work through Elidir; and blending the direct guidance given to us with the inspiration he himself received, Elidir produced the design of the Temple as it stands today. Anthony's task was to get this vision actually built, and it was perpetually made difficult by the very difficulties the firms of builders we employed got themselves into, bankruptcy included. Painful birth-pangs the Temple had (coupled for us with the worry of raising such a huge sum), and it was a late birth, too, when with literally hours to spare it was ready for opening as Minesta entered her eighty-third year on 9 June 1974. A brother wrote:

> Visitors to New Lands on this day had come from distant places overseas and throughout Britain. But we were surrounded by an even greater company of radiant beings in spirit – recent brothers of the Lodge and rank upon rank of brethren of past ages, and mingling with these shining ones planetary angels, their flaming brilliance rising in spirals of light to the sun.
>
> Into this glorious assembly of universal brotherhood came the white-robed choir on earth, uniting all hearts in praise as they sang Bach's chorale 'Now let every tongue adore Thee'. And then the whole congregation rose in tribute as Mr and Mrs Cooke entered the Temple . . .
>
> Behind the altar are hung long curtains of pale yellow, as if spun from the rays of the sun. They suffuse the Temple with glowing ethereal light. In the centre of the altar which itself seems made of light stands the simple grail cup filled with liquid gold, burning the eternal flame, and above, caught in some sun-lit ray, the scintillating crystal star – truly a breath-taking vision of beauty.

Minesta and Faithful leave the Temple after the opening service, 9 June 1974

Together, choir, congregation and celestial voices (for those with ears to hear) sang 'the Old Hundredth' arranged by Vaughan Williams: 'All people that on earth do dwell' . . . White Eagle, enfolding us in his loving presence, spoke the simple words of dedication of this first temple of the New Age . . . and, as if in answer, a wonderful excerpt from Brahms' Requiem: 'How lovely are thy dwellings fair' performed by the choir . . .

White Eagle spoke with great power, sounding the note of brotherhood – brotherhood on a cosmic scale, for the earth is part of an infinite universe; brotherhood of all life on earth through conscious co-operation between man and the angels, man and the natural kingdoms; brotherhood and peace among men, for we are all one in spirit. The key to this universal harmony is obedience to the law of love.

As our Gentle Brother so inspired our vision, the sun streamed across the downland, through the amethyst windows, bathing us all in light. A shower of rain had blessed the Temple and in the distant rumble of thunder we heard echoes of the voice of God. The elements had indeed shared in the consecration of our Sun temple.

What could follow but Parry's 'Jerusalem'? . . .

Tenderly Mrs Cooke, looking so young and so lovely, brought us back to earth with her heartfelt words of thanks, on this her most joyous of birthdays. And she urged us all to go out into the world and create more Temples of Light to guide humanity into the new age.

STELLA POLARIS, *August-September 1974*

The opening in fact was done twice over! We had so many applications for tickets that after fitting 500 people in on 9 June, we had nearly as many more for a thanksgiving service a week later. Now it is with us, The Temple, a dream realised, a meeting place for two worlds; and no one could have been more profoundly thankful than Minesta, when at last the work of all those years was done.

TELEVISION REVIEW
Report South – the Temple at Rake. BBC South 10.15 p.m. 11 June 1974. The first television programme to describe the White Eagle Lodge was broadcast two days after the opening of the Temple . . .

STELLA POLARIS,
October-November 1974

Frequently I walk with my husband across the garden to the Temple, which is now a landmark over a wide area of the Hampshire countryside, and there we gaze at its beauty, paying homage to the bushes and trees already planted in the Temple garden. My heart is full of gratitude for this miracle – for indeed it is a miracle, accomplished as all so-called miracles are by the steady concentration upon the Great White Spirit (God) and the power which emanates from God which brings us all together as one. The Temple is a demonstration of what can be accomplished by co-operative effort, and by trust in God.

Grace Cooke, Newsletter 1975

One good friend of the Lodge was Maurice Barbanell (Barbie), Silver Birch's medium, who had known Minesta almost since his boyhood. Over the years the Lodge had drawn gradually further away from the movement of Spiritualism as Minesta had known it in her youth, for part of its work was to try to create – as it were – the new Spiritualism. Barbie had a profound love for and loyalty to 'the Guides' as they were known – those teachers from the other side of life who were giving their profound and practical teaching through their chosen instruments on earth. It was all part of the great breakthrough from the world of the spirit to awaken men and women to the reality and closeness of that world. Barbie loved White Eagle, and he loved and admired White Eagle's medium too; this respect and affection created a very valuable bridge between the Lodge and the movement over which he had so much influence. The opening of the Temple was a proud moment for Spiritualism as well as for the Lodge. In the spring following, this pride was expressed formally when Minesta – to her intense surprise – was awarded the title of 'Spiritualist of the Year' in recognition of her work.

After the struggles and frustrations of the years the Temple was being built, Minesta found herself able to work with renewed energy after the opening, and she and Brother Faithful, both now in their eighties, were to be seen on the Temple platform each time there was a public service, giving the address or in Minesta's case serving as channel for White Eagle. But as a Michaelmas summer, once over, turns so quickly into autumn, so when Minesta's health broke in 1976, she had to cease her public work completely. The next years were ones of great testing for her, for the family who cared for her, and for the work, which missed her sorely.

As she became ill, so Brother Faithful's grip on life also deteriorated. On 3 September 1979 she 'gently and peacefully laid down the burden of her physical body and went forward, as someone has said, into the "light and loveliness she has so richly earned" through her life of service and the warmth of her love' (STELLA POLARIS, October-November 1979). Brother Faithful lived, but half in the other world, for nearly two years more, passing on 28 July 1981. It was just before 9 p.m. on the eve of the wedding of Prince Charles and Lady Diana Spencer, and thus 'just before the first beacon was lit which was the signal for the lights to spring up in a chain of fires all over Britain' (STELLA POLARIS, October–November 1981). How well, outwardly, those beacon fires symbolised the inner work Brother Faithful had done for most of his life: that of building the fire of love and brotherhood in people's hearts – especially in his own country of Britain.

ACHIEVED IS THE GLORIOUS WORK! All readers will by now know that the £140,300 needed to clear the cost of the White Temple at New Lands was finally found by 1st May 1977.

This is wonderful, and much, much thanks is owed to all who contributed and all who have helped to bring about this miracle . . .

The fund was nicely and appropriately completed for the Third Anniversary Service in the White Temple on 5th June 1977, which was also White Eagle's Service to mark the Silver Jubilee of Her Majesty the Queen.

STELLA POLARIS,
August-September 1977

A NEW INFORMATION FOLDER FOR MEMBERS
Members of the Lodge will recall that in this year's Members' Newsletter we mentioned that we were preparing a new information folder for their use; this is now ready. It is particularly designed to help isolated members participate in the service and activities of the Lodge.

STELLA POLARIS, June-July 1977

5

The Future

MINESTA would not wish us to labour her qualities – she and Brother Faithful are unsung as heroine and hero of this tale. But we will permit ourselves to observe one quality above all, Minesta's obedience and loyalty to the guidance of the spirit, whatever the cost to herself. Without such a quality, our work would never have started, could never have continued through the war years, and could never have produced that great flower it did in 1974. We will leave the reader largely to imagine the tributes that came from all sides, when first Minesta and then Brother Faithful passed.

But not entirely, for the greatest tribute that has been paid them is to be seen now in the very solid form beside the Temple, and at the eastern end of New Lands house, as we shall see.

During the great expansion of the worldwide work in the 1970s, it became ever clearer that the combination of our General Office, the room containing the Addressograph machine, and the borrowed rooms in the cottages on the estate used as personal offices, were ludicrously inadequate. One by one New Lands bedrooms were requisitioned, and sheds and outhouses round the estate converted for offices. Even then desks had to be used on a time-share basis!

This was one problem. The other was that although the Temple was operating successfully, we had had, when it was built, to abandon a second stage of the project giving more ancillary accommodation: chapels for healing groups, a meeting room for visitors, and a room for Brotherhood use. This was now becoming a pressing need. For instance, the only way to give visitors tea after a service – and some of them came hundreds of miles to the Temple – was to go over to New Lands house, in all weathers, and serve it there. The same applied for the sitters on healing groups. Moreover, the Temple bookstall was cramped, pressure on cloakrooms excessive, and the crowd after a large service impossible to fit into the tiny area of the Temple foyer.

When Minesta passed, it was obvious that her friends would want to do something in her memory. Our first thought was for the rose garden – the 'garden of remembrance' we had long wanted, and to which White Eagle had referred in his vision of the Temple. But the other needs seemed to hang over us, and one day Ylana had a very clear message from Minesta. We had to get on with the twin projects we were considering right away, while the tributes were still being paid. 'First the offices, then the temple extension.' And so the Grace Cooke Thanksgiving Appeal was launched, including the funds that had already come in as spontaneous gifts in her memory.

The Appeal got off to a head start, compared with the Temple Fund, as it began with a legacy. Symbolically, this was a very good foundation, because it was the legacy of one of White Eagle's most courageous workers, rarely in the limelight but tireless in his service, Minesta's brother-in-law Frank Wharhirst (Frank) . Uncle Frank, as everyone called him, was still 'in harness' when he passed on his eighty-ninth birthday, 20 February 1977. A large part of his life in his later years *was* New Lands, and it is very fitting that the foundation of the Appeal for the new buildings was the capital realised from Uncle Frank's house in Petersfield, which he left to the Lodge.

Leaping ahead slightly in our story, we should say that this legacy and a later one, from a Brother in the West Country, were among four larger sums received for the Temple extension. Another was a private gift, and another was a grant of £50,000 by a charitable trust on the condition that we would allocate a similar sum to match it. With interest realised, these sums represented just over half the total found. The rest of the Appeal came as individual donations – whether made directly, or subscribed through one of the fund-raising activities held at the Lodge or by one of the provincial groups – or, for that matter, the overseas ones. Many such gifts came as tributes to Minesta and Brother Faithful; but in October 1981 the Appeal was relaunched as the Golden Jubilee Thanksgiving Fund, in the hope that we could raise the amount by Jubilee Year. And we did – all £471,000 of it!

One of the fund-raising events we should like to mention was a sponsored mountain-climb. Rather evocative, it seemed, of our work as a whole, not just of the sum to be raised. The idea was to climb all the mountains in Snowdonia over 3000ft high in the space of a weekend. Perhaps it is best summed up in the words of one walker to another, when like everyone else his companion was suffering severe knee pain: 'It's at this moment it becomes not just a physical challenge, but a spiritual one as well!' A challenge the walkers responded to, and having climbed all fourteen peaks, they raised over £4000 for the fund, the largest amount ever raised by a single Lodge event. We think we hear them saying that they themselves felt the better for responding to the challenge, too.

All sorts of activities were tried, to raise funds, and we thank everyone for their inventiveness. There was a regular 'Appeal Page' in STELLA POLARIS which gave news of them all. One of the most attractive, though not always the most effective financially, was the series of concerts held in the Temple over these years. They brought to us, in addition to some of our own talented musicians, wonderful solo singers, choirs and instrumentalists.

Walking the South Downs, 1980

YORKSHIRE WALK
Our leaflet draws your attention to our sponsored walk across the South Downs . . . but you may like to know that our York and Northallerton groups are also organising a walk, in aid of the Thanksgiving Appeal, on Saturday 13 September. [This, like the South Downs walk, immediately became an annual event for our Yorskhire groups.]

STELLA POLARIS,
August-September 1980

*Work on the New Lands office extension
as it nears completion*

We are delighted that after long
delay the large print edition of THE
QUIET MIND really *is* expected this
summer.

STELLA POLARIS, June-July 1983

[Since 1983 PRAYER IN THE NEW AGE
has also appeared in a large print
edition. We have a special group
for the blind and partially sighted,
which includes a tape
correspondence scheme; and the
book SUNRISE is available in Braille.
We have also received a request
from the Royal National Institute
for the Blind to permit a 'talking
book' to be made of THE WAY OF THE
SUN.]

ASTROLOGICAL CONFERENCE AT NEW
LANDS
On 7th and 8th April the first
conference of the White Eagle
School of Astrology was held at
New Lands . . . In the evening we
were delighted to welcome Zach
Matthews, the editor of 'The
Astrological Journal' who spoke on
the history of astrology . . . This
talk was a fitting conclusion to the
conference – the first of many, we
hope.

STELLA POLARIS, June-July 1976

Another great help in being able to build the two extensions by
Jubilee Year was the fact that we had an offer from one of our
Brothers to oversee the construction himself. This not only improved
the quality of workmanship, but cut our bills as well, and there is
much for which we are deeply grateful to our Brother 'Clement',
Alex Ross. He was truly guided to leave his home and work in
Glasgow, where he was an experienced quantity surveyor, in order
to guide the building work. In the case of the New Lands extension,
which finally opened in the spring of 1984, he has personally seen
everyone comfortable in their offices, and has continued his respon-
sibilities beyond the mere construction stage with both buildings.
We thank you, Alex, and your team.

In our Newsletter that year was conveyed to all who had given
their contribution to the building of the offices the gratitude of 'the
Brotherhood in the world of light, who, because of the increased
order and harmony in the office accommodation, will be able to
give more help and inspiration to those who are doing the work at a
practical level'.

During the last few years, something of a new generation of
White Eagle books has been produced. They were not necessarily
planned as such, but that is how they now seem, and perhaps their
special task is to emphasise how the higher worlds interrelate with
this one. THE STILL VOICE (1981) is a book of White Eagle readings
which lead into meditations. THE WAY OF THE SUN (1982) talks about
the great festivals of the year and how they are celebrated in the
higher worlds; and JESUS TEACHER AND HEALER (1985) seeks to
make real for everyone that most perfect and gentle brother in the
spirit. The books have also succeeded in carrying the teaching to a
still wider readership.

A few changes in the running of the main Lodges have taken
place in the last few years. Now we use New Lands much more
fully, running short courses as well as retreat weeks. The first
Group Leaders' Conference was held in 1976 and it has since
become an annual (or nearly annual) event. It has increased the
worldwide bonds that unite the 'family' in brotherhood, to have so
many of the groups represented together. Yoga *asanas* have become a
part of many a person's life in the Lodge, and yoga courses are held
periodically – astrology ones too. An alternative type of Sunday
service was introduced in London in April 1979. It was partly a
response to the fact that it was difficult to maintain the size of
congregation every week in London after the Temple opened, and
was to take place every fortnight as a smaller service upstairs in the
Brotherhood Chapel. What has in fact happened is it has proved so
popular we are running out of chairs! In the 'New Age Communion'
as it was first called, music plays an important part in raising the
consciousness into what is ideally an act of worship in meditation.

Group Leaders' Conference, March 1984

Our Sister Radiance, who for so long had looked after the London Lodge, moved to New Lands at the end of the 1970s (and, with characteristic energy, took on many new duties there). Moon-flower, whom we have already mentioned, bravely stepped into the gap she had left and took daily charge until she too retired in 1983. In the meantime our younger generation both in the wider family and in the immediate one have been taking a greater role, not only in the Services but also in visits to Lodges and groups at home and overseas. In July 1984 Jenny and Geoffrey Dent and Colum and Jeremy Hayward were all ordained as Ministers of the White Eagle Lodge, having undergone a considerable period of probation and training in the years before.

*

And so we come to the present moment, and to our future. We have just seen the Temple extension come into use, not in Jubilee Year, but actually in time to give shelter to the special events we have been holding in Jubilee Year. How, we can now ask ourselves, could we possibly have organised them otherwise? And yet we would not have dared think, when the Appeal was launched, that they could actually be built and paid for by the end of 1985.

The Temple extension already has an atmosphere of its own, serene and somehow joyous too. Its centre (though not its geographical centre) is the Brotherhood Library, which includes books of the many religions of the world, many of them from Minesta's own collection, and houses the twelve-leaved round oak table (commissioned from the Edward Barnsley workshop nearby) which we find touches our spirits as well as our earthly senses with its beauty.

TEMPLE EXTENSION OPENS
We are delighted to announce that the Temple extension will come into use at the Easter Sunday service (4.30 p.m. on 7th April), when cups of tea will be available to all in the new meeting room afterwards. The building will have been formally dedicated in the Brotherhood service before this.
STELLA POLARIS, April-May 198?

(The meeting room was indeed used on this day, but the whole building was not formally opened until the Temple Anniversary Service in June.)

THE AMERICAS
The Lodge, as 'The Church of the White Eagle Lodge' has now been registered as a non-profit-making organisation in the U.S.A., and it is hoped that recognition by the Inland Revenue Service will now follow. So, after years of preparation, the Lodge is now firmly established in the Americas and a new and healthy Daughter is born.

STELLA POLARIS,
October-November 1983

Ylana Hayward and Joan and John Hodgson at the Golden Jubilee party, March 1986

Much attention is focused on the Americas and Australasia, where retreat centres, built on the New Lands model, are planned. But we do not think the continent of Europe will be far behind, for in Jubilee Year there seems to be a surge of activity there as well.

Jeremy and Colum visited Australia in 1983 and Jenny and Geoffrey the States in 1984 (visiting a gathering of all the American groups and members in Colorado): each of these visits was characteristic of the worldwide character our work has taken on. The Australasian centre is to be built in the hills of the Great Dividing Range north of Brisbane, overlooking virgin country; and here training in the work will take place as well as retreats. The centre will be a focus for the whole continent, including New Zealand (where the work is also growing). In America similarly, although the retreat centre site is geographically the same as the new Montgomery Daughter Lodge (designated such in Jubilee Year) it will serve two continents, as we have groups in Mexico and Brazil already, as well as those in the U.S.A. and Canada. At present funds are still needed to buy the site, which is in open country north of Houston, and like the land in Australia has not been

developed by the white man. Although each has been chosen because of the locality of the Daughter Lodge, each is a special site in itself and has some of that feeling of inner power we have learnt to recognise. In Golden Jubilee Year our own sponsored walk at New Lands is being held in aid of these projects (and a special eighty-mile pilgrimage walk to New Lands from the stone circle at Avebury, too), uniting our efforts at the Mother Lodge with those of the brethren in the New World and in the Southern Hemisphere.

Colum and Jeremy visit Willomee, our Centre in Queensland, for a retreat in September 1983. The group photograph includes brothers from Sydney and New Zealand who were there, also Mrs Doris Commins, our Australasian Representative.

*

Minesta asked me to give you this message and to ask you to open your vision and see that she is here in her gold robe. She comes with so much love for every one of you in this group, even if you do not know her . . . White Eagle, too, you will see, so full of love, so radiant, and he asks us . . . to lift heart and mind to that beautiful Star.

Now White Eagle and Minesta and the band behind them want you to know a very important truth: that for this group of the Lodge of the White Eagle something very important is happening. Minesta and Faithful, through the will of the Great White Spirit and under the direction of the shining Brotherhood, have to withdraw in their physical bodies, at the moment, from this work, but they work with us in spirit, and White Eagle wants everyone to realise the importance of this period when *a bridge of light is being built.*

Joan Hodgson, address in London Lodge, 7 August 1977

Although these words were spoken two years before Minesta's passing, it would not be inaccurate to date the current phase in the White Eagle work from the time they were given. The nature of this phase is defined in the clause we have put in italics: 'a bridge of light is being built'. In other words, we are at a stage when our most important task is to show the closeness of the two worlds and to show how – without a psychic instrument – we all can be fully aware of those on the other side of life and of the help we receive from the advanced souls there. This has always been true of the Lodge work, but at the present time the passing of our founders and leaders, Minesta and Brother Faithful, gives us an unequalled opportunity to make this truth real.

In our work the symbol of the Star has grown more and more real, as has the sense of oneness which comes with it. It is, truly, the way to the higher world. And the Temple, the earthly temple of the Star, is a place where the two worlds can meet. Increasingly, it has become a focus for workers for the Light. Many visitors have come to the Temple in the years since it opened, many just to sit and meditate, to absorb its beautiful atmosphere, and then to go back to their own path, their own work, with renewed inspiration. So the Temple has also become a meeting place between workers and

WE HAVE A COMPUTER
For some time we have recognised that the growth of the work would require us to transfer the vital records system . . . to a computer, and investigations have been steadily proceeding. Now, suddenly, we have a computer, thanks to a very generous gift, by a member, of an actual machine and supporting equipment.

STELLA POLARIS,
August-September 1985

Some of the 100 White Eagle Lodge members at the Americas Retreat in Colorado in 1984. Among them is Jean Le Fevre, our Americas Representative.

人類の秘庫を開く

ホワイト・イーグル
霊言集

グレース・クック
桑原啓善訳

Grace Cooke
"MORNING LIGHT"
"SUNRISE"
"GOLDEN HARVEST"
The White Eagle Publishing Trust
New Lands·Brewells Lane·Rake
Liss·Hampshire·England

The latest of many translations of the White Eagle books – this one into Japanese, and published in 1985

seekers of many paths, as well as between the two worlds of earth and spirit.

It is almost impossible to define the inspiration which has come to so many White Eagle workers, members and friends all over the world as a direct result of the Temple being here in visible form. It is indeed as though heaven and earth meet here. When one is in the Temple, either in the physical body or in meditation, it is easy to draw aside the veil and touch the heaven world, and to realise the oneness of all life. It is our centre, the receptacle for the inspiration and healing which radiates to workers all over the world. Each group, each individual member, is linked in spirit with the Star and thus with the Temple (which is the physical counterpart of the Star Temple in spirit), and through this link each is strengthened in his own work of radiating the Light of spiritual healing into the world. Many who have never seen the Temple find they can come in thought and be part of the work, and share in the peace and blessing which flows from it. A typical letter came to us from a new member in Nigeria: 'Thank you for the "Light" from the White Temple. Its radiance is reaching me and my people here and we are being healed all round'. Visiting members, seeing the Temple for the first time, so often feel at home, as though they have been here many times before; and a poem which was contributed to STELLA POLARIS perhaps sums up the power which the Temple has on the imagination:

> . . .I looked back at the Temple as I left,
> but did not leave.
> For now the Light illumines
> all I see and think and understand.
> We are all stars,
> made bright with love,
> and when I think of it,
> I want to dance.
> *Enid McGilvray, in* STELLA POLARIS, *August-September 1984*

*

More and more as we take the services we are aware of a Lodge in the world of spirit 'similar to our Temple building on earth, yet much more beautiful and harmonious, where the work continues in an unbroken stream' (Joan Hodgson in STELLA POLARIS, August-September 1984).

We are aware constantly of White Eagle's presence, and of Minesta's and Brother Faithful's: not only as we go about our own work but through the letters we receive from members and friends all over the world. Not least from absent healing patients, who write of remarkable experiences when White Eagle, or Minesta or Brother Faithful, has made themselves known to them; or how, through extraordinary 'coincidence' a loving White Eagle helper was brought to them at a time of need. The knowledge that White Eagle is with us was confirmed for us recently in a very evidential way when the autobiography appeared of the medium Ursula Roberts. Writing of how she is conscious not only of her own spirit guide but of others – such as Silver Birch – she told how (to her) White Eagle

> frequently appeared in a great hazy light in the centre of which was a form reminiscent of an Indian chieftain. I have seen this vision when with people about whom nothing is known to me and I invariably take it as a sign that such people are associated with the White Eagle teachings; this is always confirmed by them and accepted as a gratifying indication that this loving spirit is aware of the thoughts of the people who read the transcripts of his teachings as given through his medium.
>
> *Ursula Roberts*, LIVING IN TWO WORLDS

So White Eagle fulfils a promise that he made to us as the phase of his communication through Minesta closed: that we would never be without him, or his guidance and love. And this is indeed true. Many, we repeat, when going through a time of great stress, have felt his brotherly strength and encouragement, lifting or comforting them, helping them to see the Christ Light. We feel him raising for us, gradually, the veil on the future, showing us the way forward, helping us to avoid mistakes, pointing to opportunities, giving us the vision we need.

We end with his words, which like those with which we began were given at our Silver Jubilee, but are specially applicable now as we set forward on an even bigger chapter of our work: 'the next fifty years' – and on into the future.

> The Age of Aquarius is at hand, the age of spirit, the age of brotherhood, *the age of freedom*! You in this Lodge have power to lead men by your thoughts, your speech, your actions – you can become pioneers. You can impress those who are asleep in materiality that there is something finer, nobler, grander, more lovely and beautiful to live for. That life does not stop when man changes his coat at death, and that the physical body need not grow weary with materiality, falter and die; instead with the coming of the Christ light into man's heart, the body becomes spiritualised. Then you will no longer grow weary but be full of joy; Jesus, we are told, danced the joyful dance of spiritual freedom, spiritual happiness, spiritual harmony. Oh, life is grand, my children, for those who have attained freedom in spirit!
>
> Surrounding this Lodge at this very moment, you will see a Temple, not built of physical matter, but of the shining substance of love and light. Over this earthly Lodge are spread two immense wings. This is the protection that is yours, the guidance

A NEW LEAFLET ABOUT SENDING OUT THE LIGHT
We have produced a new leaflet incorporating the words of our prayer for 'Sending out the Light' and giving directions on how to use them to pray for a peaceful and beautiful world. We feel this challenge of projecting the Light is something in which many who know nothing about White Eagle but long to help and heal can be encouraged to join in, and the new leaflet is suitable for anyone who believes in God and the power of prayer. It's called 'There is something YOU CAN DO – NOW'.
STELLA POLARIS, *April-May 1985*

that you have from the Lodge above. Do your best, my children, and do not fear anything earthly. God's Angel Messengers are very close to you, helping, ever inspiring, guiding you when you yourselves choose the right and the true way of life.

We would draw you all together in this Shining Temple of Light, the perfect Lodge above, where we can see the perfectly laid stones which went into its building. The builders, who are they? Yes, the Brethren who followed the Light of Christ. You yourselves are young apprentices; but nevertheless are helping the masons to maintain this temple in the heavens. The Grand Master is there, waiting, enthroned in golden light. He draws you close to Him.

In this world go forward unafraid. Keep on keeping on. The early Christian brethren of the Piscean Age served faithfully. You are Brethren of the Aquarian Age, and you too must serve; and vaster possibilities are before you.

May the Great White Spirit bless you.

*The round oak table in the Brotherhood
Library in the Temple*

APPENDIX I: White Eagle Daughter Lodges

Some of our Daughter Lodges have been mentioned in the text, but as it would too frequently interrupt the narrative to list them all there we now append a short note about each. We wish that space permitted us to account for each White Eagle Group, too: but their numbers are too great. As White Eagle's prayer has it, 'All service is valued and all are equal'.

EDINBURGH, Scotland
An Edinburgh group of the Brotherhood has met since the beginning of 1935, but the Daughter Lodge was dedicated on 30 March 1940 and was the home of the Lodge as a whole late in that year, after the bombing of Pembroke Hall (see main text). With the opening of the Daughter Lodge the Edinburgh brothers moved from 8 Rosebery Crescent to 98 Hanover Street, where they remained until 1948. Since that date the Daughter Lodge has had various homes: the current address is c/o Ranald Godfrey, 46 Inverleith Row, Edinburgh EH3 5PY.

GLASGOW, Scotland
The Glasgow Lodge opened only two years later than its sister at 58 West Regent Street in 1942. There has always been a strong group of White Eagle workers in Glasgow, and great has been the faith in which they have worked, but the Lodge has had its vicissitudes in the sudden loss of both premises and leaders. Glasgow reverted to the status of White Eagle group in the late 1970s, but we are delighted to share the news that now, in the summer of our Jubilee Year – 1986 – Glasgow has once more become a Daughter Lodge.

NEW JERSEY, U.S.A.
Opened on 17 August 1947 (see main text), this was the first overseas Daughter Lodge, although there had been Groups abroad – in Nairobi, for instance, since 1936. The first Lodge was at May's Landing but meetings were held in Atlantic City also.

Although the New Jersey Lodge could not continue actively much beyond the mid-1970s, it will always be the first Daughter Lodge of the U.S.A., and the torch has been handed on to other White Eagle Groups there.

BOURNEMOUTH, Dorset, England
The Bournemouth Lodge has its origins in the group which met in Christchurch, Hants., in the 1940s. It became our third U.K. Daughter Lodge in April 1952 and transferred to The Hurst, 7 Leicester Road, Poole, Dorset BH13 6BZ, where its meetings continue to be held today. It celebrated its Silver Jubilee in 1977.

PLYMOUTH, Devon, England
'The first meeting of the Plymouth Group was held at 7 Woodside on 11 January 1952.' So says Retrospect 1956. The first Brotherhood meeting was held on 7 February 1954, and the work has continued in Plymouth ever since. The Lodge moved to the north of the city in 1963 where it overlooked the edge of Dartmoor, and it now meets at 72 Bickham Road, Higher St Budeaux, Plymouth PL5 1SB.

WORTHING, Sussex, England
The sanctuary of our Worthing brothers was dedicated by Minesta and Brother Faithful in July 1959 although the history of the Group goes back to 1954. Much valuable work was done but in the 1970s the Worthing Lodge was without premises, and activities slowly ceased after the passing of its leader in 1971. Seeds were sown of groups elsewhere, however, and today a new White Eagle group is operating in Worthing.

ASCOT, Berkshire, England
White Eagle dedicated the Ascot Group sanctuary on 18 March 1961, and the Group was listed as a Daughter Lodge from December 1962. Activities were held at Broadmeads, Coronation Road, until 1965, and brothers from Ascot are still active elsewhere in the White Eagle work.

READING, Berkshire, England

The Reading Group goes back to 1959, but became a Daughter Lodge when its premises in Oxford Road were dedicated by White Eagle on 24 April 1962. The Lodge soon outgrew its premises and those to which it moved in 1967 were actually bought for the Lodge by individual contribution and form part of the Lodge Trusts. This building, the home of the Reading Lodge to this day, was dedicated on 4 October that year. The house has a garden around it and our Reading Lodge has been well tended! The address is 15 Erleigh Road, Reading RG1 5LR.

THE HAGUE (DEN HAAG), Holland

A Daughter Lodge formed in The Hague with the move there in July 1965 of the Group that had met in Wassenaar since 1962 or before. On 16 October 1965 it was opened, under the name 'Stichting Witte Arend Centrum', when White Eagle dedicated the sanctuary at 37 Pomp-stationsweg (see main text). Sorely tested by its leader's ill-health and her passing in 1968, the Dutch Lodge through its gallant leader was a symbol of courage in adversity. Although the Daughter Lodge had to close, the White Eagle work is carried on strongly and faithfully at an increasing number of groups in Holland.

EPPING, Sydney, Australia

'Our Group, which as you know became a White Eagle Group under the leadership of the late Mrs Winifred Browne, is still carrying on as enthusiastically as ever': so runs a letter from the Epping Group leader in STELLA POLARIS, October-November 1961. We name Mrs Browne because she was the 'acorn' from which the 'tree' of our work in Australia grew. The great undertaking of the Group was the building of its own chapel, completed in 1969, an act of great faith. The faith has been justified, for although the Lodge had to close in 1973, and its premises were eventually sold, the bequest of the property is the foundation of our plans to build a retreat centre in Queensland.

So the work in Australia has a continuity from the very early days of the Lodge. Today we have five groups in Sydney, too far apart geographically to have formed a Daughter Lodge yet, but very much together in spirit.

EXETER (and TEIGNMOUTH), Devon, England

A White Eagle Lodge was dedicated by White Eagle at 14 Buckeridge Avenue, Teignmouth, on 11 October 1971. Its leaders and members worked faithfully there for fourteen years and it was only in 1985 that the move was made to Exeter, chiefly to give the Lodge a more central base. Much has been created by our Teignmouth/Exeter friends, not least the virtual rebuilding of a stable cottage to be the present Daughter Lodge home. This was dedicated for White Eagle by Ylana and Colum on 20 October that year, and the address is St John's Cottage, 87 Polsloe Road, Exeter EX1 2HW.

CROWBOROUGH AND BRIGHTON, Sussex, England

The formation of a Daughter Lodge from the group at Crowborough in June 1975 was a natural progression: for as our 1974 Newsletter states, public services were already attracting a regular congregation of 35-40. Since the Crowborough leader moved to the U.S.A. in 1982 the activities of the Lodge have been shared by the various groups of which the Daughter Lodge is composed, and public services have been held in Brighton (at the Unitarian Church, New Road) since 1979 and later in Tunbridge Wells also (at the Friends' Meeting House). For newsletter of activities write to Mrs Reta Harrison, 8 Milnthorpe Road, Eastbourne, Sussex, BN20 7NN.

IPSWICH, Suffolk, England

The Ipswich Daughter Lodge was founded on 8 November 1976, but its earliest history is in Bury St Edmunds, where the Brotherhood had met since 1968. When the Ipswich group began shortly after, the two worked in harmony, and the creation of the Daughter Lodge in 1976 was an expression of the unity of East Anglian groups in four counties. Fifteen Inner Brothers were present when Ylana dedicated the premises that year. The Lodge, at Flat 4, St Edmund's Lodge, 57 Henley Road, Ipswich IP12 4DD, is in a pleasant position overlooking a park; the chapel, seating about thirty, shares the simplicity of the New Lands Temple.

BRISBANE, Australia

A Daughter Lodge was appointed at 33 Longland Street, East Brisbane, early in 1976 and the work was carried out there for a number of years. In

1982, however, the Lodge moved north of Brisbane, into the hills, where near the township of Maleny its work continues to grow. The advantage of the country setting is that as at New Lands retreats and courses can be held, which is specially useful as the Brisbane leader, Mrs Doris Commins, is also 'mother' to all our groups in Australasia. The country centre is called Willomee (after White Eagle's valley, described in THE ILLUMINED ONES), and it is here that a purpose-built retreat centre is planned. Some activities are still held in the city itself. For all details write to The White Eagle Lodge (Australasia) Ltd., Willomee, M.S. 16 Tesch Road, Maleny, Qld 4552. A regular newsletter is sent out.

MONTGOMERY, Texas, U.S.A.

Montgomery is our latest Daughter Lodge, created in our Jubilee Year at this town north of Houston. As with Australasia, the leader of the Daughter Lodge is also our official Representative, and it is in the country around Montgomery that it is hoped to build our retreat centre for the Americas.

There are many groups throughout the Americas, and the running of the work across the continent is done co-operatively, though the bulk of it rests of course with our Representative, Mrs Jean Le Fevre. For regular newsletter and details of activities write to The Church of the White Eagle Lodge, P.O. Box 8182, Montgomery, Texas 77387.

Daughter Lodge leaders at New Lands in 1983. From left to right, standing: Leo Lane (Reading); Ranald Godfrey (Edinburgh); Colum Hayward, John Hodgson, Jenny Dent, Irene Hancock ('Radiance'), Noel Gabriel (Lodge solicitor); John Kemp (Ipswich); Geoffrey Dent. Seated: Betty Jones (Reading); Dorothy Wright and Joanne Atterbury (Exeter and Teignmouth); Doris Cooper and Agnes Shellens (Plymouth); Joan Hodgson, Ylana Hayward; Eunice Dixon (Bournemouth); Barbara Tracey (Ipswich).

APPENDIX II: Short-title Bibliography of the White Eagle Books and Associated Publications

Not included in this list; unprinted teachings, pamphlets, catalogues, photographs, posters, correspondence courses, newsletters, foreign translations, gramophone records, tape cassettes.

Fuller details of books to 1957 are given in A BIBLIOGRAPHY OF THE WHITE EAGLE PUBLICATIONS, W.E.P.T., 1958; and of current publications, in our illustrated catalogue.

*Indicates that a book is out of print and may only be had from secondhand bookshops, or on loan from the Lodge libraries.

The initials W.E.P.T. stand for The White Eagle Publishing Trust and the place Liss, Hants. Books are cloth-bound unless stated (the term cloth is intended to cover all styles of hardback binding). Later editions share the publication details of the previous entry unless stated. An editor's name is added where there is a significant amount of editorial text.

A. *Serial Publications*

*1. ANGELUS. The White Eagle Lodge, London.
Monthly except August, June 1936 – October 1951 (until November 1939 inclusive, in duplicated typescript). Continued as STELLA POLARIS.

2. STELLA POLARIS. Grace Cooke and Associates, Liss, Hants; from February 1954, W.E.P.T., Liss, Hampshire. Bi-monthly, beginning with the December issue, December 1951 to date.

3. THE WHITE EAGLE CALENDAR (variously thus, A WHITE EAGLE CALENDAR, or THE WISDOM OF HAPPINESS WHITE EAGLE CALENDAR; and variously The White Eagle Lodge, W.E.P.T., etc.). Annually, 1944 to date (actually published in the autumn preceding).

B. *Books associated with the White Eagle teaching but not published by Grace and Ivan Cooke, The White Eagle Lodge, White Eagle Publications, or W.E.P.T.*

*11. THE GOLDEN KEY, Ethel Welsford. Arthur H. Stockwell, Ltd., London, [1929].

*11a. _____
_____, second edition, retitled KEY OF GOLD. The Society of Communion, Erlestoke Park, Wilts., [c.1933].
[A series of letters from George and Percy Welsford to their mother Mrs Ethel Welsford, through the hand of Grace Cooke.]

*12. WAVES OF LIGHT, written down by The Scribe. Privately, from the London Spiritual Mission, [c.1930].
[A series of White Eagle teachings recorded by Mrs Robertson Rogers.]

*13. THY KINGDOM COME, arranged and edited Ivan Cooke. Wright and Brown, London, December 1933.

*13a. _____
_____, second edition. December 1935.
[For later editions see no.123, THE RETURN OF ARTHUR CONAN DOYLE.]

*14. LITTLE POWDER-IN-THE-JAM TALES. Ivan Cooke. Wright and Brown, London, [October 1934].

*15. THE LAW IMMUTABLE, Ivan Cooke. Wright and Brown, London, January 1935.

*16. PLUMED SERPENT, Grace Cooke. Rider and Co., London, June 1942.

*16a. _____
_____, The Psychic Book Club, London, September 1942). [See also THE ILLUMINED ONES, no.133]

17. THE WHITE EAGLE INHERITANCE, Ingrid Lind. Turnstone Press, Wellingborough, Northants, June 1984.

See also no. 116a. Note that editions and titles by Rose Elliot (vegetarian cookbooks) other than those published by us are not listed here.

C. *Books published by Grace or Ivan Cooke, The White Eagle Lodge, White Eagle Publications, or W.E.P.T.*

*101.   THE HEAVENS ARE RINGING, Ivan Cooke. Privately, Wembley Park, Middlesex, [1930], paper.

*101a.   _____, second edition, W.E.P.T., February 1966, cloth.

*102.   [A LITTLE BOOK OF PRAYERS] No title. The White Eagle Lodge, London, February 1937, paper.

*102a.   A LITTLE BOOK OF PRAYERS. Second edition, April 1940. [See also nos. 112, 125].

*103.   ILLUMINATION, Volume I, 'given through "W.E."' The White Eagle Lodge, London, [July 1937].

*103a.   _____, second edition, March 1940, paper.

*103b.   _____, third edition, October 1946, as 'The Second Book of the "Illumination" series', paper [THE OPEN DOOR, November 1946, now being scheduled as the first volume.]

*104.   'THE PRESENT WORLD CRISIS' AND THE KARMA OF NATIONS, 'White Eagle'. The White Eagle Lodge, London, December 1937, paper.

*105.   WAYS OF SERVICE IN THE WORLD TODAY, 'teaching of the White Brotherhood' [White Eagle]. The White Eagle Lodge, London, [February 1938]. ('Illumination Series').

*106.   THE CHRISTIAN MYSTERIES, 'as given through "W.E."' [edited by Ivan Cooke]. The White Eagle Lodge, London, November 1938. ('Illumination, volume II').

*106a.   _____

_____, second edition. White Eagle Publications, London, November 1943, paper.

*107.   THE WHITE BROTHERHOOD, [Ivan Cooke, with teaching by White Eagle]. The White Eagle Lodge, London, October 1939. ('Illumination Series', Volume III).

*108.   A COURSE OF SPIRITUAL UNFOLDMENT, I, [White Eagle, edited by Ivan Cooke]. The White Eagle Lodge, London, June 1942, paper ('Illumination Series').

*108a.   _____

_____, second edition, July 1944.

*108b.   _____

_____, third edition, October 1946.

*109.   SPIRITUAL UNFOLDMENT, THE SECOND BOOK, [White Eagle, edited by Ivan Cooke]. The White Eagle Lodge, London, [February 1943], paper. ('Illumination Series'.)

*110.   SPIRITUAL UNFOLDMENT, THE THIRD BOOK, [White Eagle, edited by Ivan Cooke], The White Eagle Lodge, London, March 1944, paper ('Illumination Series'). October 1944, paper. ('Illumination Series'). [See also nos. 129, 137.]

*111.   SPIRITUAL UNFOLDMENT, THE FOURTH BOOK, [White Eagle, edited by Ivan Cooke). The White Eagle Lodge, London.

*111a.   _____

_____, second edition, October 1946.

*112.   PRAYERS OF THE NEW AGE, [White Eagle, edited by Ivan Cooke]. White Eagle Publications, London, November 1942, paper. [A

successor to no. 102. See also no. 125.]

*113.   WISDOM IN THE STARS, Joan Cooke. The White Eagle Lodge, London, [July 1943], paper.

*113a.   _____

_____, second edition (revised), September 1959, cloth.

113b.   _____

_____, Joan Hodgson, third edition (revised), June 1973, paper.

*114.   HEALTH, POISE AND HAPPINESS, Joan Cooke. White Eagle Publications, London, September 1945, paper.

*115.   THE BROTHERHOOD TEACHING, [White Eagle, edited by Ivan Cooke]. The White Eagle Lodge, London, [November 1945], paper.

*116.   THE SHINING PRESENCE, Grace Cooke. The White Eagle Lodge, London, [June 1946], paper, cloth.

*116a.   _____

_____, The Psychic Book Club, London, February 1951. [See also THE ILLUMINED ONES, no.133.]

*117.   THE OPEN DOOR, Grace Cooke. White Eagle Publications, London, [November 1946], paper. ('The first volume of the "Illumination" Series'.)

*118.   A RELIGION OF HAPPINESS, White Eagle [edited by Ivan Cooke]. White Eagle Publications, London [November 1947], paper, cloth. ('The third book of the "Illumination" Series'.)

*119.   THE LIVING WORD, Grace Cooke [with White Eagle's Teaching]. White Eagle Publications, London, December 1949. ('The Second Volume of "The Christian Mysteries"'). [See also THE LIVING WORD OF ST JOHN, no. 151.]

*120. BY WHAT AUTHORITY?, [Joan Hodgson and Ylana Hayward]. White Eagle Publications, Liss, Hants., February 1953, paper.

*121. HEALING, Ivan Cooke in collaboration with Grace Cooke. W.E.P.T., July 1955. [See also HEALING BY THE SPIRIT, no. 148.]

*122. MEDITATION, Grace Cooke, W.E.P.T., November 1955.

122a. _____, second edition, November 1965.

122b. _____, May 1983, paper.

*123. THE RETURN OF ARTHUR CONAN DOYLE, edited by Ivan Cooke, W.E.P.T., 1956. [A revised edition of THY KINGDOM COME – see no. 13.]

123a. _____, second edition, October 1963.

*123b. _____, third edition, June 1975, paper.

123c. _____, fourth edition, April 1980, cloth.

124. MORNING LIGHT, White Eagle. W.E.P.T., November 1957.

*125. PRAYER IN THE NEW AGE, White Eagle [edited by Ivan Cooke]. W.E.P.T., [December] 1957. (Sub-titled 'A White Eagle Book of Prayers') [See also nos. 102, 112.]

125a. _____, second edition, much expanded and revised [edited by Jeremy Hayward], September 1978. (Sub-titled 'Prayers and Invocations of White Eagle'.)

125b. _____, large-print edition [of no. 125a], 1984.

126. SUNRISE, White Eagle. W.E.P.T., October 1958.

127. GOLDEN HARVEST, White Eagle. W.E.P.T., December 1958.

128. THE PATH OF THE SOUL, White Eagle. W.E.P.T., September 1959.

129. SPIRITUAL UNFOLDMENT [subsequently SPIRITUAL UNFOLDMENT I], White Eagle. W.E.P.T., November 1961. [Stated to be 'Second Edition' of no. 108 but in fact this and no. 137 present the material of nos. 108-111 in a different order with further teaching added, and are not directly comparable.]

130. HEAL THYSELF, White Eagle. W.E.P.T., November 1962.

*131. WHY ON EARTH, Joan Cooke. W.E.P.T., October 1964.

*131a. _____, Joan Hodgson, Second edition, September 1979, paper.

*132. THE NEW MEDIUMSHIP, Grace Cooke. W.E.P.T., October 1965.

132a. _____, 1985, paper.

*133. THE ILLUMINED ONES, Grace Cooke. W.E.P.T., October 1966. [A reprint, with some new matter, of part of PLUMED SERPENT, no. 16, and THE SHINING PRESENCE, no. 116.]

133a. _____, May 1983, paper.

134. WISDOM FROM WHITE EAGLE, White Eagle. W.E.P.T., October 1967.

*135. SIMPLY DELICIOUS, Rose Elliot. W.E.P.T., November 1967, spiral bound.

*135a. _____, revised edition, April 1974. [Published by Fontana from 1977].

136. THE GENTLE BROTHER, White Eagle. W.E.P.T., November 1968.

137. SPIRITUAL UNFOLDMENT II, White Eagle W.E.P.T., November 1969. [See note to no. 129, SPIRITUAL UNFOLDMENT I.]

*138. THE LIGHT IN BRITAIN, Grace and Ivan Cooke. W.E.P.T., 1971.

138a. _____, 1983, paper.

139. THE QUIET MIND, White Eagle. W.E.P.T., 1972.

139a. _____, large-print edition, 1983.

140. HULLO SUN, Joan Hodgson. W.E.P.T., 1972.

*141. NOT JUST A LOAD OF OLD LENTILS, Rose Elliot. W.E.P.T., 1972, spiral bound. [Published by Fontana from 1976.]

*142. THE JEWEL IN THE LOTUS, Grace Cooke. W.E.P.T., October 1973.

142a. _____, 1985, paper.

*143. THRIFTY FIFTY, Rose Elliot. W.E.P.T., 1973, wire-stitched.

144. THE TEMPLE ANGEL, Ivan Cooke. W.E.P.T., 1974, wire-stitched.

*145. ANGELS AND INDIANS, Joan Hodgson. W.E.P.T., 1974.

*146. SUN MEN OF THE AMERICAS, Grace Cooke [with White Eagle's teaching]. W.E.P.T., 1975.

146a. _____, 1983, paper.

*147. BEAN FEAST, Rose Elliot. W.E.P.T., September 1975, wire-stitched.

*148. HEALING BY THE SPIRIT, Ivan Cooke. W.E.P.T., October 1976. [A revised edition of HEALING, no. 121.]

148a. _____, March 1985, paper.

149. OUR FATHER, Joan Hodgson. W.E.P.T., 1977, wire-stitched.

150. ASTROLOGY, THE SACRED SCIENCE, Joan Hodgson. W.E.P.T., November 1978.

150a. ——————, September 1980, paper.

151. THE LIVING WORD OF ST JOHN, White Eagle [edited by Ylana Hayward]. W.E.P.T., September 1979. [An expanded edition of THE LIVING WORD, no 119.]

*152. PLANETARY HARMONIES, Joan Hodgson. W.E.P.T., October 1980.

153. THE STILL VOICE, White Eagle [edited by Ylana Hayward]. W.E.P.T., September 1981.

154. THE WAY OF THE SUN, White Eagle [edited by Jeremy Hayward]. W.E.P.T., November 1982.

155. GOD LOVES US ALL, Jenny Dent. W.E.P.T., 1982, wire-stitched. (Spiritual Teaching for Children series, Vol. 1.)

156. WHERE IS HEAVEN? Jenny Dent. W.E.P.T., 1982, wire-stitched. (Spiritual Teaching for Children series, Vol. 2.)

157. THE GIANT JIGSAW, Jenny Dent. W.E.P.T., 1982, wire-stitched. (Spiritual Teaching for Children series, Vol. 3.)

158. GREAT TEACHERS, Jenny Dent. W.E.P.T., 1982, wire-stitched. (Spiritual Teaching for Children series, Vol. 4.)

159. A WHITE EAGLE LODGE BOOK OF HEALTH AND HEALING, Joan Hodgson, with recipes by Rose Elliot. W.E.P.T., 1983.

159a. ——————, 1985, paper.

160. JESUS TEACHER AND HEALER, White Eagle [edited by Jeremy Hayward]. W.E.P.T., 1985.

161. THE STORY OF THE WHITE EAGLE LODGE, [members of Grace Cooke's family, edited by Colum Hayward]. W.E.P.T., October 1986, paper.

INDEX

Numbers in italics refer to illustrations